elizab

eridge

elizab eth eridge

ELIZABETH GORDON McKIM

A Memoir in Poetry, Song, and Story
with Previously Unpublished Poems by

ETHERIDGE KNIGHT

KINCHAFOONEE
CREEK PRESS ≈ ATHENS, GA

Copyright © 2023 by Elizabeth Gordon McKim. All rights reserved.

ISBN: 978-1-7350172-4-2

Acknowledgments:
"Beyond Words:" C.R.E.A.T.E. Vol 5, Coroboree, 1995
"Big Brown Bear:" *Wild Women of Lynn,* Ring of Bone Press, 2014
"Blues for the Trouble Maker:" *Boat of the Dream,* Talking Stone Press, 1988
"Down Home Bali Style:" *The Red Thread,* Leap Frog Press, 2003
"El Paso:" *Defined Providence,* 1993
"Evening Raga:" *The Red Thread,* Leap Frog Press, 2003
"Fish:" *The Red Thread,* Leap Frog Press, 2003
"Hey Danger:" *Lovers in the Free Fall,* Leapfrog Press, 2020
"Knife / Life:" *Soundings East,* 2016
"Listening in on Eth:" *The Red Thread,* Leap Frog Press, 2003
"Sacred:" The Café Review,
"Vision:" C.R.E.A.T.E. Vol 5, Coroboree, 1995;
"When I Hold You Dying:" *The Red Thread,* Leap Frog Press, 2003
"You Looked at Me and Spoke So Clearly:" *The Red Thread,* Leap Frog Press, 2003

"Lil Hope" was inspired by Steve Stoller's sculpture entitled *Little Hope* which we passed by each day in the Stoller Gallery window. It was chiseled out of Indiana limestone. Lil Hope is a squat and resolute household god with her wide feet on the good ground.

Several of Etheridge Knight's poems appear in *The Lost Etheridge: Uncollected Poems of Etheridge Knight,* Kinchafoonee Creek Press, 2022

www.kcpress.org

table of contents

chapter 1

Freedom and Confinement / 15

chapter 2

Invitation Waltz / 33
The Bear / 34
First Words / 35
Big Brown Bear / 37
Triple Nickel Blues / 40
Warning / 43
Elizabeth / 44
Dearly / Beloved / Mizzee / 45
Elevator / 46
You / 49
Desert Rose Stone / 50
Blues for a Lady in Boston / 51
[Somewhere in the free] / 53
Fish / 54

chapter 3

December, 1981 / 59
I Watched You / 60
[Ms E — O Miz E] / 63
[So / the context] / 64
Vision / 65
Old School Ties and Other Synchronicities / 66

On the Go / 68
Motion / Commotion / 70
October / 71
For Bett Gordon / 72
Paducah / 73
Knife / Life / 77
Chance Dancer / 79
Unfinished Sestina for Etheridge / 81

chapter 4

El Paso / 86
Juarez / 88
Pussy / 89
Eros / 90
The Knife / 92
Sometimes the Sadness / 93
Offerings and Amulets / 95
Scared / 98
[It is a bitch no break] / 100
Ruminations from the Brookline Public Library / 101
[In September 1988] / 102

chapter 5

[Out of the great wind it came] / 109
[we see / thru the / window] / 110
[Give the love] / 112
Watch / 113
He Called it "A Faraway Country" / 115

chapter 6

Therapy / 119
The Sack / 121
[Ketchup] / 124
From Interview "Freedom and Confinement" / 126
Betty Blues / 127
Angel Fish / 128
Forge / 130
Hustler / 131
Blues for the Trouble Maker / 132
Notes for a Play Called the Waitin' Room / 133
In My Lover's House / 134
Burial Ground / 135
Waves / 139

chapter 7

[Out of the tunnel into the Mississippi sun] / 143
[This mountain is vast] / 144
[When I slip to sleep] / 145
Swallowing Song / 147
During the Night / 149
Ride / 150
For Jenifer McKim / 151
O Elizabeth / 154
Beyond Words / 155
[Taped to the wall of my cell] / 158
Prison / 159
Habit / 160
Words of Fire / 161

chapter 8

[Maybe I'll meet her in Denver] / 165
Angel / 166
Entries / 167
Entry [Wanna know] / 168
Entry (Jan. 7, 1991) / 169
February 3, 1991 / 172
Entry (Feb. 18, 1991) / 173
Listening in on Eth / 175
Entry [The days roll in and out in waves] / 177
Last Stand / 179
Sunday Morning / 181
Ride the River / 183
Last Free Peoples / 185
Haiku / 187

chapter 9

Entry (Jan. 28, 1991) / 191
Death / Breath / 193
We / be / Runners – We / Free / Runners / 194
Sampson Snake Root / 196
February, 1991 / 198
February 7, 1991 / 199
Fog Clarity / 201
Sirens in the Night / 202
February 11, 1991 / 204
February 14, 1991 Valentine's Day, Indianapolis / 206
New Hampshire / 208
When I Hold You Dying / 212
Having Come This Far Away / 213

Seeing My Dead Lover in a Dream / 214

chapter 10

A Lil' Hope Is All We Need / 217
Entry [and the magnitude] / 219
[Lean close to earth] / 221
Pass / over / 222
Song Snippets / 225
[Even separation] / 226
[And continue on and on] / 227
[The way he peers in] / 228
Song / 229
Faraway / 230
Having Come This Far Passing On / 231
Deathrow / 232
Song / 234
Infant / 235
You Looked at Me and Spoke So Clearly K / 236
February, 1989 / 237
This is an Event of Hearts / 239

> —Elizabethridge
>
> There is a bridge called Elizabethridge
> Connecting two poet/people.
> Sometimes the bridge
> Would sway and dance, and bend
> with the wind;
> Sometimes it would stand, solemn
> Straight, as still as a church's steeple.

Written by Etheridge Knight on the flyleaf of Elizabeth McKim's copy of The Essential Etheridge Knight

chapter 1

About you and me and Freedom too —
'Bout you and me and Freedom too

— Elizabetheridge

Photo: Etheridge Knight

freedom and confinement

> i found you doing
> The green stick break dance
> With your old growth pals
> And your new found friends
> On the wide green stage
> Of the deep forest floor

1.

"First thing I remember is Mama teaching me to take my bread and move it in circles round the bowl to sop the molasses. And you know I've always loved sweet things, and I always love Mama, and I believe in circles," he said.

Poetry comes from memory and imagination. He remembers the pop pop sound of sweet potatoes his grandmother used to cook over a fire in Mississippi. He remembers the prayers to Allah of the Muslim brothers in the joint when they were on a hunger strike, and so was he. That chant sound moving down the cell block. He remembers his mother at the Freewill Baptist Church his last Easter Sunday, and she sitting up in the choir singing "Washed in the Blood of the Lamb," that solo sound coming on so clear and strong. "It's the sound that rattles the ear bones" he said.

The ear drums. The ear bones. Or the took / took / droom of the gandy dancers in Tennessee tamping the railroad ties when he was a boy running away from Paducah on his way to Uncle Jim in Mississippi: *down home.* And it was these rhythms that find their way into his poems, insistent as Ilu the Talking Drum. *KaDoom.*

Etheridge Knight was a natural born teacher. Everywhere he went he generated Free Peoples Poetry Workshops. It wasn't an individual thing. It was a circling thing. And this is where many young poets learned to exercise their imaginations and trust their voices. One circle moved into another and moved on out into the uni / verse, that one verse Etheridge listened to with a whole belly of feeling. He had been *called* long ago when he learned his first toasts out on the streets and parks of Indianapolis from a wino named Houndmouth. And after he did his hard time in Indiana State Prison for armed robbery where he first started writing and publishing his poems, he practiced his art all over this country, in just about every state... in prisons and barrooms and libraries and grand reception halls and schools and college campuses and the Library of Congress. *Stand up and say the poem. Take the space. Speak to us. Speak to us.*

Ask the poets in Memphis or Minneapolis or Toledo or Worcester or Philly. Or Indianapolis during those last years before he passed on to the Ancestors. Each week the poets came by for Free Peoples Poetry Workshops. Sometimes it was in the basement of the Atheneum where a year or so later the Tribute to EK would be held, bringing in poets and friends from all over the country, including Dudley Randall and **Haki R. Madhubuti**, Galway Kinnell, Robert Bly, Sharon Olds, Donald Hall, Mari Evans, Yusef Komunyakaa and others. Sometimes it was downstairs at Mugwumps, an historic venue in downtown Indy. Once, on a hot summer night, it was out on the benches in front of the Nickel (555 Massachusetts Avenue, the Barton Apartments public housing project where we lived). And when Etheridge got really sick and found it difficult to move around, we had it upstairs in 18J in the apartment. The poems were heard, the scene was charged. Sonny Bates, Herman Salinas, Elizabeth McKim, **Michaal ll Collins,** Francy Stoller, Steve Stoller, Jean Anaporte, Donita Parrish, Fran Quinn, Kenneth May, James Taylor, Gail Klein, Steve Ziliak, Evelyn Kellum, Kenny Washington, Lamont B. Steptoe, and others. Sometimes Yusef Komunyakaa would come down from Bloomington, and Mari Evans in the early days, and Sam Allen and Deta Salomé Galloway from Boston. A different group each week.

At that time, we could go to the State Museum in downtown Indianapolis and see Steve Stoller's monumental painting *Free Peoples Poetry Workshop*, and we could understand the power of the poet, the poems, and the people: that trinity which was at the heart of Etheridge's teaching. "Never forget your people, or your people will forget you." Each week he gave a mini lecture on some aspect of poetry. A ceremonial beginning. A way of entering in.

2.

First time I met him was in a bright yellow poetry book with black letters called *Belly Song* at the Brookline Public Library in the early seventies. Me: newly defined poet. Single mother. runaway white woman scraping the hawk from the sky. The book just leapt up and jumped out at me. Later on, Fran Quinn, good friend and fellow Massachusetts poet, and I got gigs in the schools in Little Rock through Mike True in Worcester. Fran said, "well if we're going to Little Rock, we have to stop off in Memphis to see Etheridge and Charlene." So we did.

But Fran missed the plane out of Boston, so I was on my way to Memphis alone. How would we find each other?" "You'll be the ones carrying poems," Fran said. It was that easy. Besides, he was a tall black man with scars on his chin wearing a red big apple cap with a nine-year-old white boy close by his side, Charlene's boy, Carl. And Charlene was from Worcester, part of my home turf. That weekend I heard that Mississippi Poet / man voice of his for the first time and the poems rolling out from the belly, and I just had to look around. I had never heard anything like that, and I knew he couldn't be stopped. He had a preacher / man authority and he swayed in a lateral motion with a forward and backward thrust in the same slow time and tune. The words came from a clear true place and the cadences stayed with me long after the words had circled and moved into message.

I don't define myself as a literary figure first, he said. *I'm a revolutionary. Try to bring the system down and turn the people around with the poems. Everything movin' in circles. And some say I'm a sweet lover and others, I'm a mean mistreater. And none of it will matter a hundred years from now. And remember Miz E, we're gonna do your autobiography, after we finish mine!*

I was thirty-nine when my first collection of poetry *Burning Through* came out. I sent it to Charlene and Etheridge. I heard a son was born: Isaac. I heard the monkey on Etheridge's back was in hard drive. Then I heard Charlene and Zack were back in Worcester. In June 1980 when I saw Etheridge again at Robert Bly's Great Mother and New Father Conference in Maine, he was alone with a palpable weariness wrapped around him. And he was drinking. I read my poem called: There is a man inside me / as terrible as myself. "Good poem, Lady, he said to me, as he leaned toward me from outside on the porch. Why did it suddenly occur to me that I had written the poem for him?

    THERE IS A MAN

    Inside me
    As terrible
    As my self
    Sometimes at night
    He scratches
    At my funny
    Bone
    And rubs
    Whispers
    Hot
    Music.
    I used to see

Him waving,
In the tall field grass
Behind my house.
He followed me
To the city
I found him
Rakin' litter
In an unspecified
Spot.
He beckoned me back
To his place
And laid me on a wood-sleek table
With a lick of a cat
I pounced
And poured him down
Like an oyster
My eyes grew round
And blissful

There is a man
Inside me
As terrible
As my self

    In November he called to say he had almost died in a fire in Memphis. Fell asleep with a lit cigarette in his hand. People in the streets shouting Poet Poet and the landlady beating the mattress with a broom trying to wake him up. Could I help him get a reading or give him a loan? I didn't know then that Eth had a list of "po poets" he called during the lean times to send him a ten or twenty or fifty (if he got lucky) to get him over. "Ol' Joe's a friend of mine. I owe him fifty dollars." I helped to arrange a reading in Boston at the Institute of Contemporary Art. On a stormy night in February he read, flanked by African American poets Samuel Allen and Sam Cornish, both living in Boston. It was a wonderful reading.

    I was with Everett Goodwin, Black poet and playwright, in February when Etheridge came to Boston. I was ensconced (he enjoyed this word which I had picked up from my mother, and he pronounced it like it rhymed with bounced). I was happy too. My daughter was just fourteen, finding the maiden she was becoming. But the closer EK got to Boston, the more agitated I got. And there was a dream. He was on his way. It was the first time. So many intersecting poems. *And some long ago song.*

> I am a young girl
> In a thin dress
> And scared

    I crossed a bridge then, and for the next decade we were always in cahoots: always dancing, holding on, letting go, coming together, troublemaking, maintaining, meddling, loving, separating, coming together again, poeting some more. I was not his first: his Alpha. I was his Omega: his last. And there were many in between. He loved him some wonderful women. And there were his wives: Sonia Sanchez, Mary McAnally, Charleen Blackburn and me. We didn't all marry the man, but we were wedded to him in our ways. And during the years there were important and beloved others. Like Deta Salomé, Lynn Walker, Akiba, Awiakta, Madeline Tiger, and White Bear. Women I have come to appreciate. There are others whom I did not know. Life friends and artist women besides. He felt safer when there were good woman around to guard his body. Like poet Carol Ann Robertson with whom he lived for several years in Philadelphia. And importantly, he was a man who loved his sisters and mama with a fierce and abiding love. As he loved his kinfolk: his children, brothers, sons, nephews, and nieces. "Being an uncle is an important office," he told me. Once he advised them on how to grow a good mustache. "Just rub on the juice of a woman. Works every time," he said, laughing.

3.

He was born in Mississippi, April 19, 1931, to Belzora Cozart Knight and Etheridge Bushie Knight. His half-brother Charles was the oldest (It was Charles in his taxi who drove him to the city limits when he wanted to leave town. "Are you sure you want to go, Junior?" he asked. "I'm sure," he said). Then there was Floydell. According to Etheridge, the two brothers were always scrapping, always fierce in their loyalties and divergent in their views, always on each other's case, even when they were grown men. After Floydell, there was Etheridge, called Junior by his family and by his nieces and nephews, Uncle Junior. Then came Clyneese with whom he had a deep bond. "Clyneese understands my situation," he says. Then Honey who was in the army and who died of Multiple Sclerosis in the early eighties." Everybody who knew Honey loved her." **Then Eunice Dale, the literary one, now passed on, who went on to write poems and plays and direct the Etheridge Knight Festival in Indianapolis.** Then baby Janice. He loved to laugh with her, tease her, watch out for her. Janice takes care of the family money matters. And there was always his beloved Mama. His father Bushie died in 1950 when Etheridge was in the army. Etheridge always missed his father, no matter what arguments went on between them.

Don't worry Miz E. I aint gonna die of cancer or phlebitis or pancreatitis or vertebrae disintegration or needle free-floating toward the brain, or no other complaint this ol' flesh can get... nope, nosirree. I'm either gonna die in prison, or by the hands of my enemy, or in Mississippi of old age. Or maybe I'll die makin' love to you. Now whaddaya think of that? So stop your worryin' woman, and let's dance. No woman no cry.

"What was he like?" a poet friend asked me the other day, "Was he a con man? Was he a kind man?" I answered, "everything you say about him, you could say the opposite, and it would all be true. Every bit of it. ('Except that I'm white, republican, and I'm gonna get out of here alive.')"

We met in New York in May 1981 after his reading, introduced by Galway Kinnell, at the Donnell Library with Indiana poet Jared Carter. We stayed in a friend's apartment on the Upper West Side. The door man from Haiti gave us the evil eye. A woman in a doorway spat and cursed us out of her baleful mouth. But we paid them no mind. It was Easter. And New York was shimmering and springtime new, and so were we. All bud-promise and lime green tree-whisper. Everywhere I looked I saw daffodils. I was wearing bright red high heel shoes in Central Park. He smiled at them often. He wore a sharp three-piece cream-colored suit. (Only time I ever saw that suit — wonder if he hocked it somewhere). We smiled on each other and found each other to be good.

Leaning on the balcony overlooking the Hudson river, he said, "this decade's gonna be ours, baby, and we're gonna have big fun and do a whole lot of poeting. Are you ready for da beah?" as he often referred to himself. A big ol' honey lovin' bear. When he waved at me from behind the glass in the limo which took him to Newark airport, I swear I saw a skull in the darkened glass, and it scared me. "Call you tonight," he mouthed through the pane.

And we did have fun. We poeted all over this country, from one coast to another, and in the heartland too. But there was always a serious drag side to the big fun. At the time, I couldn't see it clearly or what it meant: Etheridge Knight: gentle, generous, and genius poet was also Etheridge Knight addict, alcoholic, and petty thief. He had been death-dealing with the monkey on his back since he was a teen-ager in the United States Army. And that would always figure into anything and anyone who had ever been close to him. Anyone who would know deep down in the deep down, "what that was all about. Was he a kind man? Yes. Was he a con man? Yes. All ways both.

4.

That first weekend in New York he found the tranquilizers in the medicine chest and mixed them with vodka. Later it was hard for him to find his mouth. His words were sliding and bobbing on a disappearing lifeline. Everything seemed dangerous and out of control. Out on the street he staggered. "Why are you lookin' at me, Miz ee, it's a shrapnel wound. Got it in Korea and it still bothers me" he said to me. That was part of the legend. And indeed, he was wounded in Korea, but it was a "psyche" wound, as he explained it to me years later.

But this was still the beginning of the eighties and we were almost new. "I'm planning to go around the world this decade, and I want you to go with me," he said. Up in the bodegas and open-air fruit and flower markets on Broadway, he stopped and engaged anyone who would listen. Tall tales and toasts. Wagers and wonderments. Some folk stopped and took the bait, and others looked through him as if they wished he didn't exist, same way they dismissed him eight years later when he was a 'guest' at the Fort Washington Shelter for homeless men. That is, until he made it up to the stage to read "Hard Rock" at a benefit reading, and some hearts fell open in one communal KaDoom.

One side of the street people drinking expensive wine and eating fancy French food and the other side of the street, people stealing from the automat and going through the dumpsters. Red rover red rover come over come over (from children's game).

But this was the end of the eighties and Etheridge was doing his dying. I've sometimes asked why I crossed the bridge with him, turning and returning with this amazement of a man, moving with him up hill and down gulley, my burden and my blessing. Perhaps it was because everywhere he went he left stories, songs, and poems, and I wanted to be part of this motion and commotion. *Mountain yielding to the sky. Sky not wondering why.* Perhaps it was because I honestly do believe EK 'saw through stone.'" "That aint nothing," he'd say. It wasn't just Dooey Shooey, the old-timer in the joint, who had the gift. The stone was always there, and he always saw through it: between his eyes when he cried in his cell, between him and the crash of his body failing before he could tenderly receive a lover falling, and under his worn shoes moving down 'the funky avenues.' He knew stone and he reverenced it, recognized its power. He gave it more credence than he gave to wood: burning and scarring anything around him with the endless chain of cigarettes left to burn wherever he tossed them. Though I have many times heard him sing "Spirit in the wood, keep the body strong," an invocational chant from Haiti to ward off any signs of sexual weakening in older men. At least that's what he said.

Low Rider, they called him in Michigan City (Indiana State Penitentiary) when he moved on up there from Pendleton Reformatory, leaving behind a lot of scared white boys who owed him from poker games. Before he defined himself as a poet, he wanted to be like George Raft. Tough guy. Ladies man. Hustler. Big time gambler. Pimp. "Lotta guys were afraid of him, 'cause he was so smart," Chuck White from prison days told me. "No one could outsmart Black Knight."

There were those who saw him comin' and got out of town fast, and others signed up for the duration. Etheridge traveled all over the country doing his poetry, and in all the watering holes, way stations, poetry towns and ports of call, he touched people, rattled their ear drums, changed their vision about what poetry was all about. Etheridge was hard on his friends, but he loved them hard too, and as he said in one of his poems, "I never stopped lovin' nobody." And that's the truth. I was lucky to know some of these friends, and I appreciate mostly all of them. For each person he engaged along the way, he was someone to remember: brother, uncle, father, son, lover, trickster, meddler, teacher, troublemaker, hero, cell boss, friend, and essentially: Poet.

"Somethin' happens when you name someone," he said to me.

I was with him in November of 1990 at the VA Hospital in Indiana when they told him what they had first diagnosed as pneumonia was terminal lung cancer. "I feel like I've been given a death sentence with no reprieve," he said to me a few days later, when the reality of the prognosis got to us, and the tears started to roll. We had just found our way home to each other after a year and a half apart, because of downward spiraling addiction which led to real damage: forged checks and shattered trust for me, and for him, six months in New York filled with bad times and broken agreements, three weeks in a shelter for homeless men, a run-in with a car when he was walking across the street in Philly, an accident that left him with a mangled leg and ongoing complications and infection in the hospital in Indianapolis all through a long and agonizing 1989 summer, and other sure signs that the life was near insane, and the streets were very scary now, Eth had sent word to some of his buddies: If anyone should ask / tell them I'm still around / tell them I'm runnin' with the wild ones / tell them I'm freedom bound." But that was mostly bravado, because there was little pleasure now and mostly pain and paranoia, desperation and depression. Monkey on the back was diggin' in for the long haul.

5.

The weather has changed. It is now winter 1991, and time is stretched thin and taut. There is nothing to spare. Only the measured breath. There is a war on when Etheridge Knight is dying. We wake to it / we sleep to it / we cry to it / it in / forms / this Gulf War: Bush's clean hygienic laser beam objectified stealth scud smartbomb war. Just like Mr. K says — the little war inside reflects the big war outside. We hold each and weep: we love we play we sleep we wake we begin again we fight we tend we make amends we abide we let slide.

But there is an enemy under the roof of the skin — beside the heart and making in / roads into the ol' liver. ("Gotta watchout for the ol' liver") Doctor Sylvia Dennison, Eth's primary care doctor, tells me an artery is wrapped around the tumor. "It could burst at any time," she says, "and if that happens, there will be a lot of blood, and he will die very fast. "Just so you know," she says. "I don't want you to panic. You are the Primary Care person. You are the person who has to know."

Gwen Brooks slips into the bedroom with Mari Evans the day the war is almost ever. She sits beside him. She kisses his eyelids. He opens his eyes and sees his dear friend and *womantor,* (in contrast to mentor) raises his head up, looks at her, smiles, looks at her again, and says "How ya doin' Gwen? and closes his eyes again. He sleeps, keeps sleeping — he will never finally wake up. A few days later, early in the morning with only Miss Belzora and me and Etheridge in the apartment, Sonia Sanchez enters quietly. Etheridge is sleeping in the living room. Miss Belzora and I are still in our nightclothes. We talk little and in soft tones. Three women circling this man who has always played the numbers: alpha, omega, and mama, all with birthdays that go in sequence: September 9 Sonia, September 10 E / liz, September 11 Miss Belzora. A final Blessing of the cosmic lottery for Mr. K: Alpha: Omega: Mama.

It is also a time when the children come home to see their father. There is Etheridge Bambata McAnally Knight, home on personal family emergency leave from the Navy. (Miss Belzora laughed and high-stepped up and down like a teenager when she heard the Red Cross was bringing home her baby boy's eldest son.) We had worked hard through the Red Cross to get him here. Then there is Tandiwe Mary McAnally Knight: his "beloved of this land." She takes the bus from Tulsa, where her mother: Etheridge's second wife, Mary McAnally, lives. Then there is Isaac Bushie Blackburn Knight. Comes with his mom from New England. It is important to know they come home to be with their father. After a long and large space of years, they hold him. He holds them. They say things. They do not say things. It is a time of blessings in a time of war.

Bam in those final days and hours kneels in the corner of the bedroom holding his father's hand, reaching out to his father at the gate, guarding his father across the farthest gulf. Tandiwe, pretty, vibrant, and strong as a wild tropical bloom, makes spaghetti for her dad and friends on her first night in town. ("Just took over the kitchen," Eth says proudly.) and later on she celebrates her twenty-third birthday and brings laughter and stuffed animals and multicolored balloons And stories. Some of the stories are tender, and some are terrifying, and everything is included here at the Triple Nickel. EK's second son Zack comes with his mom Charleen for Thanksgiving, and he doesn't want to leave. He has the finely chiseled features of his mother, and the wide-open heart, brown skin and broad chest of his dad.

There are things that can never be said. "Be careful in the telling," Eth reminds us all. Still, it is important to know that the children come home. Each one has his or her experience of this time. It is not for me to tell. It is only important for me to tell my experience. That is all I can do.

At 11:00 AM on March 10th he went to the "Faraway Country," which was how he referred to his death. It gave us a way to talk about it. "Now lady, what's going to happen to you after I go to the Faraway Country." He even suggested that I join a church, so I could meet someone suitable for me. Here I had to laugh. We laughed quite a lot during these days. And cried some too.

Etheridge dies in my arms, surrounded by family and friends in Indianapolis Indiana in the Barton Apartments for Elderly and Disabled people, 555 Massachusetts Avenue, affectionately called the Triple Nickel, or sometimes just the Nickel: home: on the eighteenth floor 18J with a penthouse view of the old midwestern city.

> I hurt in certain
> Places when the wind caves in
> You die in my arms

That ours was the relation / ship of two poet people: one displaced Black Mississippi poetman one displaced white yankee poetwoman is not without meaning. As I titled my poetry cycle creation story, Mud Matters In The First Circle, we were both deeply ensconced in the Oral Tradition of Poetry: we both felt the sounds and the dance and the language at work in ourselves and in the people and in the uni / verse. We were both doing our poeting in the community, both Free People doing what we do in our various ways, and all ways listening to the messages. As he told me we would, we rode the river together all the way to the sea. And just as he said in those final hours, the earth is continuing in its circular motion. And just like the rhythms of the wind and the tides, the phases of the moon, and the passage of the seasons, the commotion continues and will continue long after all of us have moved to the faraway country.

And now I lightly mention the angel of death. I barely say the words. Only that he or she was in the room and she or her was relentless. Miss Belzora felt the angel, too. Later on, after it was all over, we talked about how Etheridge and I fought our hearts out. We swatted. We flailed.

This is the fourth go round. I am ready to move on now. It's time. I need to, and I know Etheridge would want me to. I have named what I know as best as I can. I have taken the time to tell the stories and I was careful in the telling, as he advised. And now I want to let it rest ah men and women. *Thanks for everything blazing.*

> Happy traveling. You'll be freedom-seeking....
> till time and time are gone to glitten.

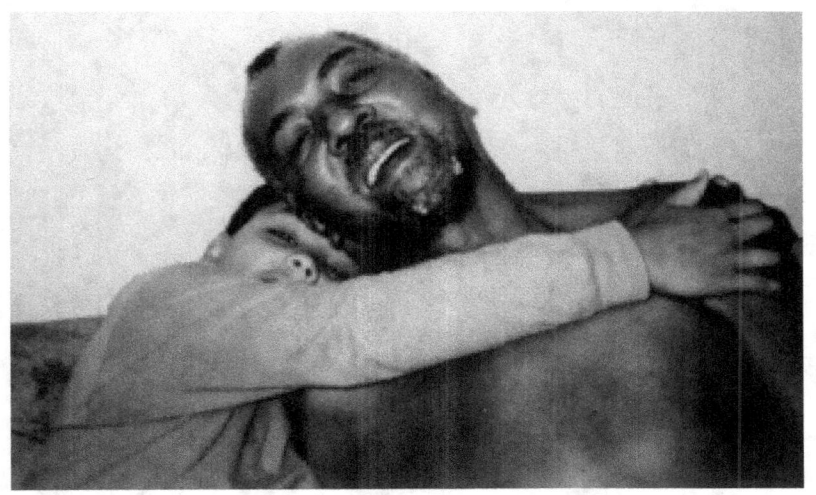

Etheridge and Isaac "Zach," 1990

Father: Etheridge Knight
Mother: Charleen Blackburn Knight

Mary Tandiwe McAnally Knight
Etheridge Bombata Knight
adopted children of Mary McAnally and Etheridge Knight

> If I can touch the future
> If I can catch the falling curve...
>
> — Etheridge Knight

2

chapter

invitation waltz

Come in around *the friendly fire*,
my love, breathe free;
and hold these poems a while, for you
and yes, for me.

It's winter here,
we seek a warming trend,
Look, we've moved past the end
and last year's war,
but even now, the wind has rubbed
us sore; the babies cry, the wild dogs
bark, scud missiles tearing up the dark.

Begin this poem, my love,
for you, and yes, for me,
It will not save us, or drag us
from the dark, but we can use it
as the children did the crumbs
to cut a path to lead us
where we **cannot** see.

Come in around
the friendly fire, my love,
breathe free. And hold this poem
a while for you, and yes for me.

the bear

I met him on the elevator of a Public Housing
Project for elderly and disabled in Indy.
Not India. Indy. Indianapolis. Nap / land. He said
He was the bear. Before I asked him, he said
He was the bear. I wouldn't have known, but
He was dressed in skins. Bear skins.

He looked raggedy and torn apart, and his fur
Was slurred with berry juice. He had the space
Around him all to himself, 'cause no one would
Go near him, up close. Not that they weren't drawn
To him, but we were all, and I include myself,
A little scared. No one said nice day. Or this
Elevator sure do stink of berry juice. Nothing
Like that. We were quiet for the whole ride.
Which was unusual. Till we got between
The seventeenth and the eighteenth floor. Then
The elevator stuck and held. Groaned. Stopped.
Stopped

Art by Phoebe Bly

first words

Finally, he spoke. "I'm the Bear. Moved back here from somewhere else. Maybe move away again. What do you want?" He looked at all of us.

I got courage. I pressed in and the words came out. "Give me the skin of one summer blackberry wrapped in bear fur. That's it," I said.

He looked at me hard through those bluey / brown eyes, squinting to take me in and hold me. Then he began to smile, a slow ride the river kind of smile. "Who you, and whatchoo doin' lookin' for a mojo?" The elevator bounced and shook with people jostling and nodding, laughing.

"It's not like that," I said, primly. "It's something for me to hope around. Like a prayer, like a circling prayer."

He looked at me again. The elevator was getting hot. People were beginning to rub up against me, to thump and mutter. I was sweating up a storm.

"So," he said. "Something to hope around. Berry skin in bear fur. Lord," he sighed, as if lord was a long way up and faraway, "why you need that?"

I looked at him straight out, straight in. Then I answered. "Long ago I had something like that. When I was a kid. Had it in my pocket. Next thing I know it was gone, and the pocket gone too. And I knew something was over. Then you arrive on this elevator on the way to the eighteenth floor. So now I remember what I lost and what I want from you."

For a moment we're as close as contact paper and shelf, and we can't tell which is which. Then it's over.

"Who do you think I am, Miss Lady? Santa Claus? The Miracle Worker? Sides, I got my own damn trouble to attend to." He brushed something off his left shoulder and turned away from me abruptly.

But not before he slid something into my hand: something he knew and I knew we both had been wanting for a long time, for a good long time. That's how I first met the Bear.

big brown bear

When they lowered you into the ground, man,
You had me second-guessed, man,
Down right / deep / pressed, man

Let us hold each other and sing I said
Let us sing to each other and hold on you said

Be careful in the telling, you said
Be telling in my care, I said

I see you wheeling down the airport corridor
Smoking in no smoking

This is the lair of da smokin' beah
Enter ye who dare

I remember 2 weeks before you died
When your mama moved in with us
How you said to me:

The earth
Has no beginning
And no end
The earth all ways
Be
Here

And I'd heard you say it before
And now it was more important

And I knew
You were also talking
About you and me and all of us
And the big eee
Earth
Forever and ever
Even though you were going
To the faraway country
You would still be here
Part of the eee
The ear
The earth

By this time
We had *"pledged our troth"*
I chose it
You espoused it
We had pledged
Heart / seriously
E and e
So we were ready

Even though we faltered
Here and there
There and here
We were riding the river

All the way
To the sea

triple nickel blues

Black knight poet and the poet's poet woman
The pair who wheels the rubber dolls in the baby carriage
The vet who mutters gook gook at three am
The blindman clasping yellow movie tickets stubs
Sol who runs the third-floor convenience store
Plays coon / can in the lazy afternoons
Chaplain Jack who listens to the Triple Nickel Blues
Lou when he comes out from under beat up cars
Undertakes tender care of his ninety-year-old dad
Hattie Mae who used to run a jook joint on Indiana Avenue
Mr Tongue who drinks with Eth beside the Frosty Tap
Marva Jo who brings us cracklin' bread
Mellow Man and Funky Drum and the Trembler
Buddies from the big top Eth's old school
Tom who likes to hear a woman sing a good catholic tune
The gray-haired white dude who calls himself Indian
And copies numbers off the wall out back
Mississippi and Ice Water and Good Kid
And the frontbench crones and cronies
And Tony and Tim in wheelchairs
Tough guys once now paralyzed from shoot 'em ups
Tim who says I'm permanent when Eth says I'm terminal
And Betty who controls the downstairs desk
And throws out danger signals junkies drunks and loudmouths

Chorus:
Where are / my meds / my wheels / my keys
Where is my check / where are my grandbabies

Isn't it time to have a pig roast?
Isn't it time to laugh?

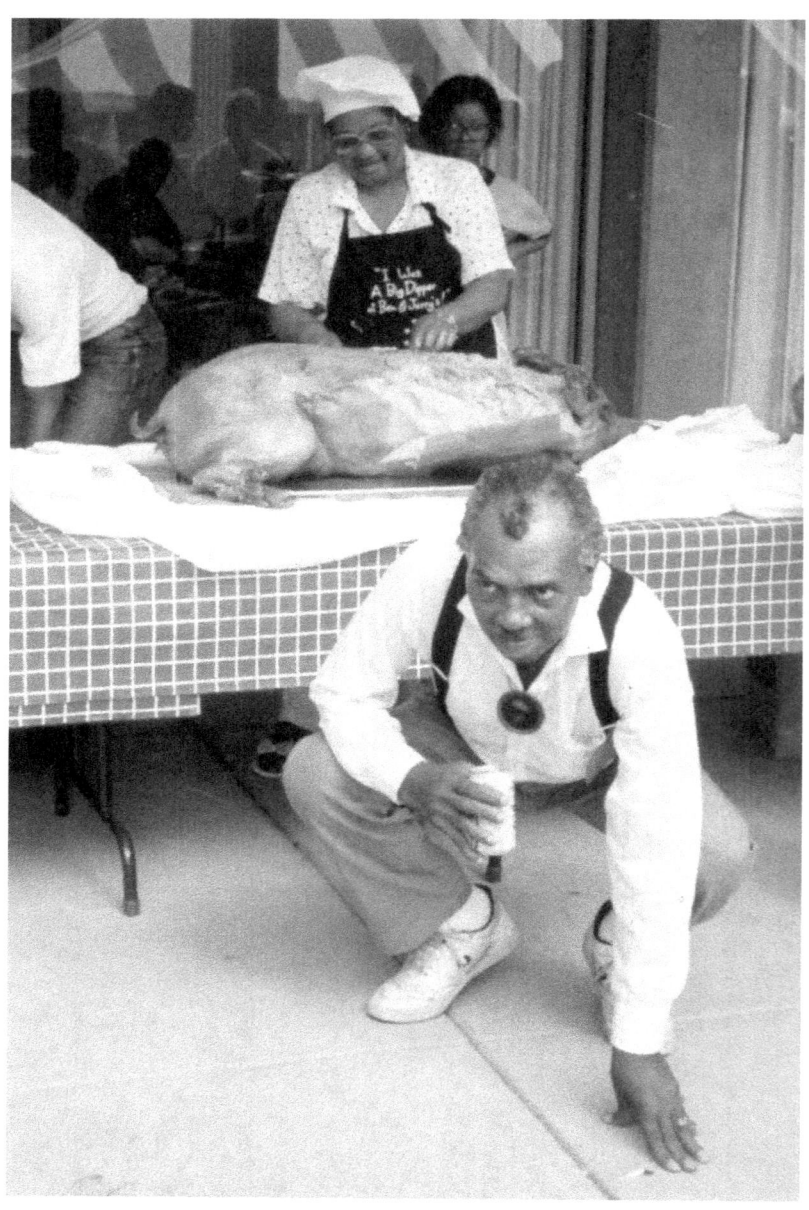

Pig Roast, 555 Mass Ave.

Photo: Elizabeth Gordon McKim

warning

This / is / the Lair
Of "de smoking Bear"
Enter Ye / all who dare
To breathe this polluted air
(— But, for truth, and for Fair,
It ain't no / worse in here
Then it is out there.)

— EK

Sign on door of what we called the Crooked Room
at 108 Winthrop where Eth did his writing

elizabeth

I got your / good / letter, and I *heard*
your voice.

    It will / be / alright, Lady. The Spring
will come soon.

    My family and I / are / still grieving
for the death of my sister.
    I understand your need for time.
    I, personally, want to look / into / your
eyes soon.
    — Gotta / be / in Omaha on the 19th —
Will call you from there.

    O Boston lady — take care of
yourself. I love you. I could ride
the river / with you / all the / way / to
the Sea.
    I want to —

        Be well
        — Etheridge

        1/11/83

dearly / beloved / mizzee

For Elizabeth Gordon McKim

Dearly — Beloved — Mizee —
I know that / this surprises Thee —
That / this honey-loving Bear
Rumbled outta his lair
Here
In ye olde Framingham
To detective you unaware,
With your white / ass / bare
Cavorting with an / other / Sam —
Bo Diddly, do-wop-de-wop-wop.

O I / do love / Thee; and if you should / ever / stop
Loving me — my blood would jam
In my veins; my breath would take
Leave of my lungs, rattling, flop-flop-
Ping, like a slave in chains;
My knees would tremble, my hands would shake
Like a Memphis crap-shooter wooing Chance;
My heart would quiver, and break,
Like a Florida oak in a hurricane.

So, I'm glad (and oh so sad) that you're gone
Away from your free and easy home.
So I'm walking this dark and green path alone —
Making this sad, and silly, poem —
Singing our blue, and true, romance.

— *Etheridge Knight*

elevator

We gain strength
Now we are dancing in the place
where river meets sea
My dad taught me the love
for growing things
tendrils and buds
loam compost mulch
green pushing up
sturdy stalk
blossom
inspected
I talked to the flowers
I watched their cycles
participated in / respected / their arrivals
and departures
daffodil and narcissus
bleeding heart
dark vulva of peony
crinkle of poppy
bridal wreath
bloodroot
dogwood tooth
slant of light
robinspeak
grosbeak
cool feel of grass
on bare feet
monarch / butterfly / newly hinged / on milkweed
crow / call / red / breast / wake / up
here in the triple nickel

555 massachusetts ave indianapolis napland nap
the elevator rises and falls
like the tides
people crowd in
and crowd out
blindman / old woman/ leaning on her walker
young blk. dude with cap acey-deucy
earphones snapped in
chaplain jack makin' a personal call
'cat' callin' out to the men
swearin'
'if this damn elevator don't move
no faster i swear
i'm gonna pee myself
i swear i will'
and the crowd nudging and jostling
except for john
water-logged on thorazine
he can't do anything
but nod

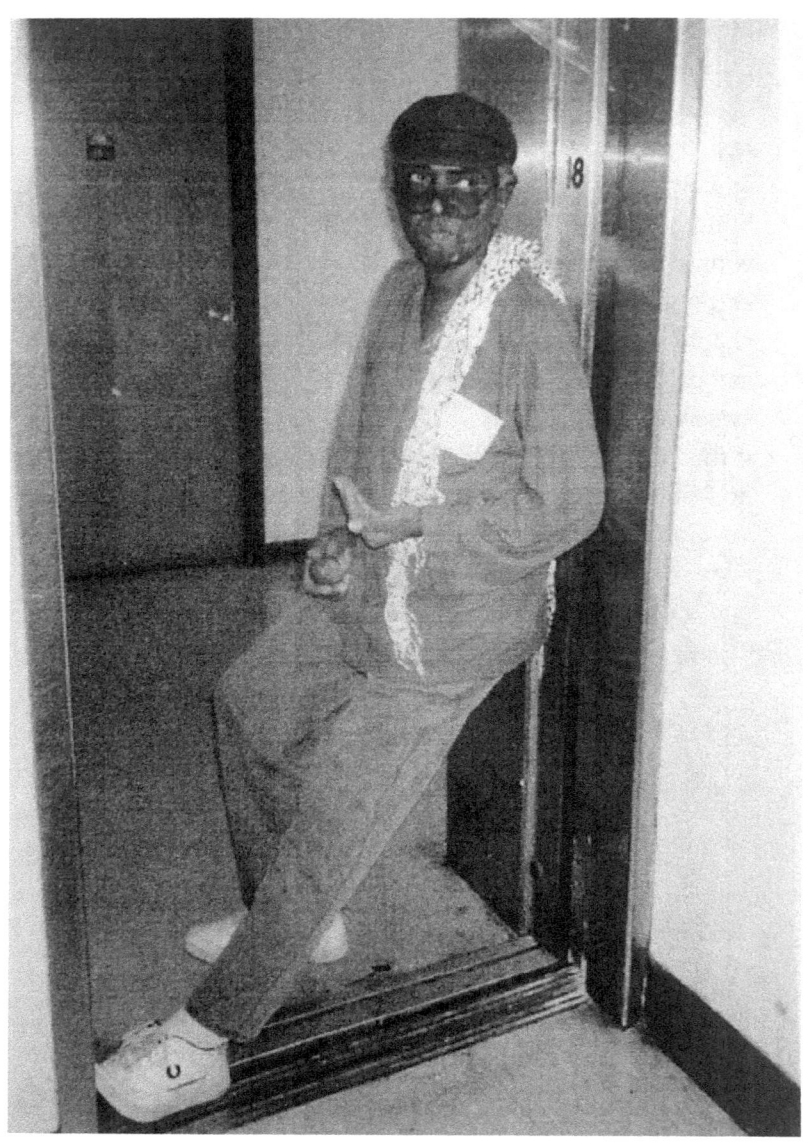

*In front of elevator and 18J 555
tasting plum and salt*

Photo: Elizabeth Gordon McKim

you

Burst forth
Unexpected like milk-
Weed into
Windy   salt-
Talk
Plums
The plain
Song   torch
The touch
Ch ch
ch

desert rose stone

Now you call me
Threnody. Not sure why
Or why you pass me by
So easily, dismiss my gritty
Surfaces, my thumb print ID
My earth works, my homely mug,
My breast plate, my flowering, my bells...
I have been here so long
There is no end
To my passage of *plums and salt*
Salt and plums.
Listen
To our song:

I take the threnody
You take the melody
I take the remedy
You take the waltz

blues for a lady in boston

I went to sleep last night with your voice ringing in
    my ears,
Fell asleep last night, o your voice ringing in my
    ears —
well, you sounded so lonely — and o so full of fears.

I woke / up / this morning just about the break of day.
O the day was dawning when the Furies started to
    play.
Thinking about you in Boston — o so faraway.

O I get this jones every time you brush your hair,
Said I get this jones every time you brush your long
    brown hair,
I know this love of mine / will / follow you every
    where.

So let's boogie in Boston, let's scream and shout,
    let's do —
Let's dance and sing and make our dreams come true.
        (softly)

About you and me, and Freedom too —
'Bout you and me, and Freedom too.

                              Etheridge Knight
                              Summer, 1981

41 Market St., Venice Beach, CA where Eth and I stayed in Director Tony Bill's studio, and Eth gave a reading at 42 Market St.

Photo: Elizabeth Gordon McKim

[somewhere in the free]

Somewhere in the free
Waters you splash up with-
Out advance notice...

And you never fail
To blind me with your blackness
Before the great fall

fish

When you first arrived
at Indiana State Penitentiary
in Michigan City
that's what you were
fish
you had that fresh / fish smell
you had that fresh / fish look
and you had to watch your fresh / fish back
and when the others came up from Pendleton
the young militant blacks
and you watched
and rejoiced
that's what they were
fish
but a new and dangerous breed
voicing Revolution
by that time
you were in love with fish
you had your own tank
in your cell
and you fell *in love* with fish
In the beginning you had the tank for the light
so you could read your way deep
into the night and sink solitary
and reckless into fanon
and malcolm and aj rogers and haki madhubuti
langston and sonia and gwen and dudley
bly and louis untemeyer's anthology of modern poetry
the title said so slowly and deliberately
you could taste the syllables

and later you fell in love with the fish
You liked to watch them swirl and glide
and sometimes when you were casting out of the pen
and angling for a flip / tail swish of a thought
you would open up your prison / vision to the fish
and you knew you were in love
in love with the scent and the ink
in love with the fish
nosing their way up against
the common glass

3

chapter

december, 1981

I'm sitting at McDonald's
Where all the crazies come:
The old, the unemployed, the immigrants.
The exiles. It is 10 AM.
I write to you.
Seventeen pilot whales washed up
On Nantucket. One was saved.
They flew it to Connecticut
Do you hear my cry?

Shadows hide
In the mystery of crannies
Where anything might be born
Momma pushes towards babe
House upends toward light
Sky drifts toward moon
Moon anchors us in water
Sisters and brothers
Gallop down the night
As day in December
Collapses, breathes, rises
Collapses again

i watched you

I watched you
  Coming toward me
    Carrying shopping
      Bags in both hands

Bearing fruit + food + fortune

I've never seen you from this view
  Before — from the 18th floor
  Window of our project apt.
You looked so small

    — Etheridge Knight

Excerpt from a napkin Eth wrote on.
Fall 1990, watching me from our
555 Massachusetts Avenue "Triple Nickel" apartment.

View from 555 looking down at the crossroads

Photo: Elizabeth Gordon McKim

The AMERICAN POETRY REVIEW

Oct. 31, 1984

BOARD OF ADVISORS
Louise S. Abrams
Dannie Abse
Seymour Adelman
Yehuda Amichai
Cathy Apothaker
John Ashbery
Margaret Barringer
Ann Beattie
Richard Boyle
Robert Coles
James Dickey
Margo Dolan
Craig Eisendrath
Mrs. Maurice English
Thomas Fleming
Carolyn Forché
Mariam Garfinkel
Meg Givnish
Barbara Greenfield
Donald Hall
Daniel Hoffman
Galway Kinnell
Etheridge Knight
Maxine Kumin
Stanley Kunitz
Norman Mailer
Mary McCarthy
Samuel Melnick
Robert Motherwell
Sondra Myers
Elnor Newbold
Cynthia Ozick
Philip Roth
Frederick Seidel
Jerome J. Shestack
Ted Solotaroff
Otto Sperr
Rose Styron
Emily Sunstein
Kenneth Tyler
John Updike
Robert Penn Warren
Ted Weiss
Muriel Wolgin

Ms. E. — O miz E.,
— Can't you hear me /howling/ down
your name? The sound, the sound
Of the wind in my ears
doesn't blow
     the same — as before...
--- a winter/thunder now rolls across my shore.
  Don't you love me anymore? — O
— Elizabethridge, Lady of my autumn dream/years
I'd leave the humming of your heart, the blow,
  — O the great blow-blow of your breath;
And the arching bridge that your motion
And your magic make; from the very start
   Of our love it has / been / so!
And in our love there is no death!
      — Etheridge

P.S. I found Ted/Jean's phone # in the
   manila envelope you brought down.

The American Poetry Review is a nonprofit organization

[ms e — o miz e]

Ms E — O miz E,
Can't you hear me / howling / down
your name? The sound, the sound
of the wind in my ears
does not blow
the same as before...
a winter thunder now rolls across my shore.
Don't you love me anymore? — O
— Elizabetheridge, Lady of my autumn dream years,
I desire the humming of your heart, the blow
— O the great blow blow of your breath,
and the arching bridge that your motion
and your magic make; from the very start
of our love it has / been / so!
And in our love there is no death!

— Etheridge
Oct. 31, 1984

[so / the context]

So
the context
of me and thee
elizabetheridge
and our separate and inter / secting
stories

I know
I have collapsed at certain places
along the map and meadow
and caved in
and in and in
and billowed out
conspicuously
and sat down perplexed
done the dog / day / chores
laughed in the wrong parts
shaken / over / and over
where sobs wrack the faraway
shores

So that is the context...
how grateful I am to have received
the messages
the context of rhythm and pulse
kadoom / kadoom
the wide sweep

vision

I saw you today
in the white congregational church.
You were sitting where my dad used to sit
before he died. You were sweating.
Your eyes were lollygagging.
Couldn't tell if it was booze or pills
or something else. You were singing willow
weep for me / way you do / and every now
and then you would howl 'where's my woman
where's my sweet woman' and the congregation
pretended you were not there. They had whited out
your fine pink tongue, your black face, your brown
eyes with the tell-tale blue rings, your bend-
back fingers, your acey-deucey hat. They knew
you had not come this way, not for hundreds
of years. Still, when you sang willow weep for me
with that deep / mississippi / poet / man voice of yours
full force / and open / they just had to look around /
they tried to cover / your blackness / with rock of ages
but it didn't work / you kept on singing / you didn't
care / ol' rev got nervous / you didn't care
it was snowing / in new england / you didn't care
the sound reached my inner ear and rattled
the bones / you kept on singing / you didn't care

old school ties and other synchronicities

In the early fifties she was going to the oxford school for girls
and her daddy's rule was golden in hartford connecticut
under the sign of eisenhower and the traveler's umbrella
and she was wearing a grey flannel blazer
emboldened with a school insignia
and optimistic cheer
while his streets were blazing
with fury and fear
when she was memorizing edgar allen poe
he was in big windy chi / ca / go
staring at the world from a flophouse
or an abandoned car
or living at the taft hotel
with a big blues woman big may-
belle and may was singing at the crown propeller
and may was hooked and so was he
while she was being permed and girdled tamed and taught
to do the waltz to sing false notes he was already
displaced and dancing to another drummer learning the ropes
of penal farms and county jails and copping dope, while she was
babysitting little blond kids through hot new england summers
and filling dance cards with serious pale boys weighting to fill full
their father's shoes, he was runnin' round town forging checks
and dodging more dangerous news more serious blues ricochet-
ing off staccato bebop sound while she was jitterbugging and
conjugating french verbs and she didn't like elvis on account of
his pelvis and she was bringing in tollhouse cookies for the over
sixties club downtown and she was readying for college oh she
was earnest and longing for love

oh he was earnest and reaching for life
he ran with a knife to keep the heroes back
he was gaining on some sharper knowledge
in the joint his old school and when graduation came round she wore
a white organza gown
and carried twelve blood-red roses while his black
blood was flowing underground
with no guardian angel to respond
to his black sound
comin' / round
say no guardian angel to respond to his black sound / comin'
round

on the go

He was on the go.
He had people to meet
poems to poet
arguments to argue
loves to love
toasts to tell
dope to cop

The man was on the go

bootlegger / va hospital / frosty tap / crap game / free peoples
poetry / workshop / college campus / stoller gallery /
walker casino / mama / sweet woman / triple nickel

but slow
he went slow
he took his time
(his time... not yours)
most times he went very slow
unless he was running for a train
or bus or plane or running
from someone who wanted something
he didn't want to give up
or toward someone
he loved with a huge heart-
busting passion or running back or
forward not wanting
to explain why he cut out
or got over or disappeared or reappeared
or saw a man about a dog.

Other / wise he went slow.
That was his style and fashion
and he couldn't be stopped.
But most times
he liked to assume the poet's position
(on his back)
and I too know
that poets need to assume
the poet's position for long periods
of time (our time not yours)
'cause it is true
we think better that way
(Junior told me so)

"Just cause I talk slow
don't mean I think slow"

He loved the poet's position
and assumed it often
preferably
with a true believer
by his side
(And that's the truth
I testify)

motion / commotion

(for two voices)

I like to mosey
You like to mill

You like to rumble
I like to spill

I like to gallivant
you like to gamble

I like to sally forth
you like to ramble

I like to hushaby
you like to drum

you like to signify
I like to hum

I like to gadabout
you like to layabout

I like to glide about
you like to slide about

I like to drift about
You like to stream

You like to roustabout
I like to dream

october

you say
our love
be the kind
that don't
run out

good
I say
'cause I be
damn tired
of running

the day in boston
soft / so soft
winter will never
happen here:
gold
just gold
falling
soft / so soft
up and down
the avenues
of trees
I think of thee

love
— e

for bett gordon

She comes to me
This Wild Woman, bringing
Flowers + Music + Revolution
(And Trouble) And
The serious mysteries
And love. And golden shoes —
          (And the blues.)
And circumlocutions
And a twirling and a Whirling
And a bringing of Breath
I love her.
To my Death.
Which is a whirling and twirling
And bringing of Breath.
And my sisters + Mother Circled
Her In Jubilee.
Yessiree.

— Etheridge Knight

paducah

for Etheridge Knight

In Paducah in the early forties
you shined the farmer shoes
all caked with mud
for one thin dime.
Sometimes those men would kick
and cuss and do things
which made you feel
ashamed. alarmed. afraid.

"Little black boy
shinin' shoes
in the south is easy
to kick as a cat," you said.

Later on
after you became a poet
you dreamed of opening
on the avenue (any avenue)
*Free People's Poetry
Workshop and Shoeshine Parlor.*

In November 1986
when things got confused like always
and your stuff from the gig
in Syracuse got sent back to Boston
in a green plastic sack going round and round
abandoned on the Baggage Claim
and your woman sailed your hat *out* when you sailed it *in*

You got yourself a rented room in Roxbury
and a j.o.b. shining shoes at Logan Airport
(so you said)

After ten days they fired you
Said you were too slow too old
Said it couldn't be helped
just too old and too slow
for people on the go
Airplane folk you know
You responded *Fuck you*
and took the trolley back
to your rented room in the berry

Too much prison
too many poems
between you and Paducah
when you snapped that cloth
over muddy farmer shoes
and felt the weight of tears
the loss of breath
and *choked / choked / and choked*

And sometime later
you read your poems somewhere
for real money and a room full of people
who listened up and never could forget
the freedom-seeking and the free
soul you *in / voked evoked in / voked*

2.

Poeting poeting
out there poeting
the word gets through
the message rises up
your mama is right
it is a calling
even when you're high
or sick or tired or cold
or feeling old
or out of sorts
it's poeting
sailing out coming in
to port its poeting
getting the message out
taking the people through
the pain and the suffering the suffocating
the in / justice the long dank hours
the march to the sea of vision
the revision the remembering
the image / nation's clear song
the freedom-seeking for the folk
looping them with a joke a story a lie
an admission a confession
"Anyone else want to cop out?"
Getting the people
into the poem
into the message
changing the fire
breathing the air
hauling the water
to the ear

earth breath
and eth
you were right
"In our love there is no death."

knife / life

when you were busy with your dying
i left it by mistake
in the bed
on my side
after i had pared the plum
and fed it to you
bit by rosey bit
and later you found that knife
in the bed
and brandished it
to 'keep the heroes back'
waved it through the air
like a commanche warrior
same way you brandished it
when you ran down the long corridor
at the indianapolis central post office
federal agents running out from their offices
yelling "stop that man stop that man"
and later on
after your mama had moved in with us
you asked for the knife
and francy and i gave it to you
mama said
"you crazy?
no tellin' what fool thing
he might do with that knife
'cause he's sick
and i don't want him wavin' no knife in the air"
and she was right she almost always is
but still

when you waved it
when you brandished it and flourished it
i knew you were gaining on the angel in our room
you were gaining back control
before the storm and strife
began to roll into our little life you waved
that paring knife and sliced the air
and listened to some formal
music there
and carved a prayer to lil' hope
and that's the truth

(and that's the dope)

chance dancer

I don't feel
like I got cancer
I feel like a dancer
and tho' there's not much music
what li'l there is
I use it.

— *Etheridge Knight*

The first time drug / wash
flooded you with ease and light
after that you got high

to escape the down / pain
which ran you on the ragged streets
till you done / *doin'*.

Political prisoner
in America you be
come a chance/ dancer.

During your illness
war begins. Ends? Desert storm.
A / wake. Iraqi Freedom?

You tell me, Mister
K, 'cause you're the one who burst
the whole damn orange!

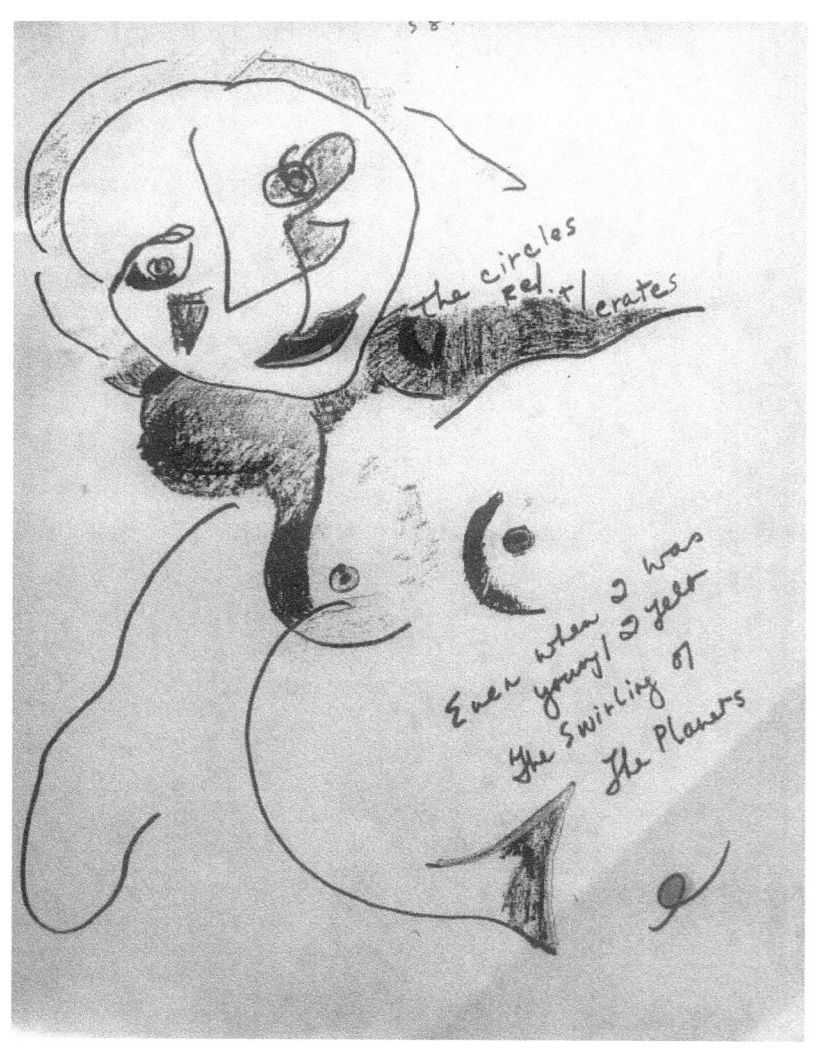

Drawing: Elizabeth Gordon McKim

unfinished sestina for etheridge

We're off to Minneapolis
and I'm scared, Eth
Look, I'm taking the air
in great gulps, I'm tasting fire,
I'm lifting off from earth
I'm not wasting a single breath

and for me everything is breath
because we're going to Minneapolis
(in my mind it's India or the end of the earth)
Let's hope you'll be there to meet me, Eth
Don't fuck up or I'll snuff the fire
and forget about taking the air

Though you know I love this fair,
this festival between us, this magic breath,
or I wouldn't be enroute to the fire
in our room at the Holiday Inn, Minneapolis
and to you, K, tracer of lost persons, Eth, Ether-
idge, nudging me back to the black belly of earth

the deep rich return to earth
(forget about air)
Now it's in the flesh of me Elizabeth
and you Etheridge in our breath
that's why we're off to Minneapolis
that's why we have chosen fire

which makes and breathes more fire
which can not always warm the earth

which is why I have flown to Minneapolis
which is why we have to take care
of what we make, which is ours, elizabeth-
eridge, this wise and excellent *Elizabetheridge*

4

chapter

Jungle beasts we be
Delicate temporary flowers
Binding promises

About you and me and Freedom too —
'Bout you and me and Freedom too

— Elizabetheridge

el paso

In El Paso the sun
urges us to praise this sweet time
these big ol' mountains

We laugh / and cry / give thanks
to all that breathes and bears
fruit / we plant / black seeds

All night / we fly / high
and nod toward each other
harvest lore and loss

We drive by day through groves
of pecans / acres / of cotton in bloom
onion and chili fields

What do we know / of
spirit / knife / life / we did not
know before you called?

Please! Let us begin
again / and end what we must
in music / and dance

Hey! Let us drink strong
healing waters / let us sing
chants for the passage

for the out / flung trip
faraway / hummingbirds / slice
green / gold / bands of air

We search our scorched mouths
for prayers / we mine the love
yield / yield / yield once more

juarez

Aug, 29, 1990

I sip corona
Beer in sun-drenched Juarez.
My lover shops, smiles, shops.

— *Etheridge Knight*

pussy

Show me the sweet pussy
what can i do i always show you the sweet
turned out she was fee / male and had kittens to prove it and
sometimes for the fun of it I would call her charlotte
le chat the french way
at night she would slide down my apartment hallway
on her backside as if it was an amusement park joy ride
but by day she was distant and removed from tom foolishness
often in those last days on the ear the earth you would
kiss my mouth touch my hair reach for my breasts
show me show me and i did reverently slowly and with
    much care
what do we know of sky or window / what do we know of
    bird or
sea / what do we know

eros

Hey babe! Hear me now
Insist on you while all falls
In the sieve of wind

Temperature dives
Land locks itself uptight
Barometer falls

Kadoom. My man returns
Intimately known to me.
Should I run for help?

Southern bear lumbers
Home up and around my trail,
Roots for hope n' honey

I've always been moist
And a sucker for love. Out
Pourings. Hidden Springs.

Unbutton my silk blouse.
Two small wonders fall out in-
To your honey paws.

Sweet dick stirrin' up
This bastion of composure
Soooo inisistantly

I greet you softly
And slowly wake you rising
To my mouth's morning.

Please my purr tongue per-
Suasively per/suade me now
Till I sing for you

Lil' love button
Sing praises to the goddess
In all languages

Don't fool me lover
I know you want to rise high
Enter/quick/sink/deep

Wild puss in the woods!
Red poppy gapes in the dark
Forest... beckoning....

We are not alone
Beside us the spirits walk
And smile on our life!

the knife

Once I bought a knife
a beautiful enamel handled razor-sharp paring knife
Bought it in Chinatown in San Francisco at a poetry gig
(the one you missed 'cause you were too messed up / to come /
down / and over and across)
the enamel handle painted with delicate embellishments:
curling red blossoms and smoking blue dragons
and curving green vines
I put it in my blanket drawer for safe keeping

Then I noticed it was missing
I knew you had taken the knife
to arm yourself for the forays
into the projects to get the rock
you were blowing your life away on

blow / blow / all the way
to crownhill / cemetery / in napland
blow away boston blow away philly
blow away new york memphis toledo minneapolis chicago
blow away mississippi
blow away baby

I ain't one of them suicide poets
poetry is about revolution
and celebration
and freedom-seeking

truth is / you is / truth is / you ain't

sometimes the sadness

Goes through me
like a knife
re / runs an egg
on the edge
of the horizon
wedged.

Dennis in the wheelchair
says "Death is easy
as opening a door."
"Oh yeah?" says Eth,
"I'll send you a postcard
from the faraway country
and let you know."

Sometimes the pain
is so great we can not hold
each other.
Our fingers pop
open
old betrayals
like walnuts.
At night
we wake up
in our own castoff
shells, telling
our true
tales:

wing it wing it
round the bend
out the window

offerings and amulets

Indianapolis, 1991

shells and trinkets
basket woven with wild vines
red ribbon from a summer straw hat
graduation medal from martin university
(an earned degree)
marbles / stones / pieces / of wood
mask made from speckled
feathers of a guinea hen
a budding gardenia plant
a flaming cyclamen
herman's chicken soup
peaches and plums from the open market
dropped off by francie and steve
a clear crystal from jean
bam's home baked cookies
a sari from india
a mexican blanket
a woven afghan
from a maine housewife
a pink amethyst shaped like a heart
from a stranger at the brookline crystal store
natural spring water from france
a hat from senegal hand stitched
a robe from morocco
a cane from haiti
a blk and white checkered kaffiyeh from abdullah
a hand made leopard skin hat from
richard in colorado old friend from the joint

birds flying overhead the american flag
the star and crescent
the sword of fire
letters and cards
turbulence whirlpools
the tremble of leaf
the pop of blossom
a red flower
faces
old portraits
my ma miss millie
your ma miss belzora
handsome and proud
athletic
traces of red kites skitter
in cornflower
blue
I jump up
you sit down
we circle
chanting
The ground sings
hymns swell and valleys sleep
the wind yields and sails off
another way
the last stop
the city limits
the frontier
a new currency
we pass
we sail through
the days and nights
birds veer

around the murat temple
we free people
build a temple

scared

Till the last breath
and that kept you moving
through the dance and de / cadence of america
'cause you were too desperately scared
to stop. Even in those last few days on earth
when you said I desperately need
to shit or when you were sixteen
and you desperately needed to get away from paducah
so you joined the army or when you were dying in the
    winter of '91 and your morphine and
dilaudid pills were stolen more than once
and you were desperate there would never be enough
and you were scared and sacred
and running since the early days
laying up in the jailhouse with a man who murdered his wife
cut off her head and you still a boy
put in jail for stealing a radio in illinois
with baby cisco and ed mac / donald
scared and sacred
now I'm up here sitting
by the st. george river maine
watching the blue heron stand on one leg
and listening to the birch leaves twitter
and i think of thee and me
as i fall asleep into a basket of stars and meteor showers
and i wake into a bucket of blue
i turn this way and that minding the breeze
and watching the little bitty brown moth shudder at my
    window
today i saw its shadow cross my book

i'm sitting and staring for the two of us
scared and sacred
in the hoop of the world

[it is a bitch no break]

It is a bitch no break
A purple mysterious bitch
To make a poem in this Library
The ghosts of poets escape book covers
And hover over my shoulder
And snitch to their god of the dead.
Their words are not much read here.
Their memories rust in the mold.
I am alone and cold.

Besides, I am covered with the cloak of Jah
All the gods I follow are women
And they are all living gods
When I seek just one
I look into the eyes of my mother
Or the eyes of my lover.

— *Etheridge Knight*

ruminations from the brookline public library

Lil' lost wonder of the bitter world
if you were here, o here
suckin' on my titties way you do
eatin' my pie with the same relish i taste the neopolitan pastry
surreptitiously in the brookline public library
damn where are you anyway
in front of me a man
reads about geraldine ferraro
in glamour magazine
don't you ever do what you did id id
last summer
sometimes it gets too much for me
and i have to kick it uphill
o i wish you were here
hey diddle diddle
in and out
the library
we make our bodies

1984

[in september 1988]

In September 1988 on the road for poetry readings and teaching, and also to assuage my anger and sadness at Etheridge's addictive behavior, I filled a year with poetry events, readings, and teaching. During that time, I went to Memphis on my way to teach in Reno, in Lesley University's Creative Arts in Learning program where I worked with teachers from all over the US, helping them to weave poetry into the school curriculum. It was there, while visiting Awiakta and Paul Thompson that I had this dream, and remembered it during Desert Storm, the first Gulf War, and the final days of Etheridge's life.

Awiakta is a special friend of ours: poet, teacher, mentor, friend, and mother, an Appalachian First Nation woman born and raised in Oak Ridge Tennessee at the time when scientists were trying to unravel the secrets of the atom. She is now a respected and beloved Nation Mother and Poet of the Cherokee. I feel this teaching dream was a vision gift from her to me and Etheridge, preparing us for what was ahead.

> Awiakta bids me sleep
> in the Dwell
> a special room in her home
> with wall paper of bending pine boughs
> which reminds her of her first home
> in the Smoky mountains
> in Tennessee
> I have been on the poetry road
> for several weeks and I am tired
> She lights a candle
> She prepares a place
> for me to sleep

and I dream:

Awiakta brings me and Eth
to a lake
she enters a bathhouse
made of pinewood

There are three diving suits
red blue yellow
hanging on wooden pegs
she dives
over and over
diving and surfacing
(though later she told me
she hardly ever swims)
wearing the suits
of continuance and change
first things
first she says
an infant crawls up the hill
like a salmon swimming home
as Eth and I
two / step down the hill
perfectly
in sync.

Totem animals here
mountain lion / owl / moose
groundhog / honey bear
red tail hawk
crawling king snake
grandmother spider
red fox and hare

turtle and turtle
dove
yak and emu
orangutang / gorilla
kadoom / kadoom
scarlet flame / bird
sturdy sun flower
i hold a small shell
little creature little creature
the water tells
eternal tunes
buck and wing
grapes in a cluster
for a small moment
i forget the threat
of clusterbombs
blackberries hide
in the thicket
i have always danced
deep / digging
rhythmically
pleas
supplications
time
weathers
whether
or knot
lungs
collapsed
tents of
breathing
fire
numbed

extremities
laundry on line
pulling in
pushing out
grow i whisper
to gardenia buds
still furled and fueled
with promise
red kite in blue sky
what do we know
we did not know before

Because of his drug and alcohol addictions, Etheridge and I were separate for about a year and a half between May 1988 and November 1989. In the spring of '88 he continued on a downward drugging spiral, left the Boston area in the wake of forged checks and broken contracts, went to New York for poetry work, landed in a homeless shelter in Manhattan for a short period, was run over by a car and damaged his leg, went to Philadelphia and stayed with friends: the artist and poet Jerome Robinson (murdered in 2001) and Philadelphia poet friend Lamont B. Steptoe. Etheridge eventually returned to Indianapolis and entered the hospital in the summer of 1989. There, he got a bacterial infection from a leg wound stemming from his run-in with an automobile. It was November of that year, in Indianapolis, when I visited him, after a separation that had lasted about a year and a half. A week after I arrived, he was diagnosed with lung cancer.

5
chapter

So often
I soften

When felt
I melt

— *Elizabetheridge*

[out of the great wind it came]

Out of the great wind it came
Laughing and crying down the long corridor
Of night into the seven syllables of dawn
Into the push of day it came
Out of the endless night it wept
Bearing bullet holes like badges the great
Wind swept pocking the sky swarming
Out the sack of particles fleeing
and flocking / fucking / the matrix pushed
Between parcels and prima
Materia aggregated reaggregated integrated
Disintegrated parakeets and paracletes comfort animals
Rescued and sheltered redefined airborn
Refined into the seven syllables of day it came

[we see / thru the / window]

we see
thru the
window
of the world
our lair
is here
and there
a bit of bone
a strand
of hair

— Etheridge Knight
Scrawled on a piece of paper

A bit of Bone.

A strand of hair

[give the love]

Give the love
The lasting pleasure
Give it
In full measure
Find the fruit
Be at the special spot
Beat the drum
Be here
Be there
Again and once again
Bear it
Wear it
We are it
What else have we got
We do
We do
We do desire it

We are scared and sacred
We are scared and sacred
We are scared and sacred
In the hoop of the world

And the green goes over and over

watch

In the cusp of loving
I skim lonely
In precise places
Near your home.
I watch you
From up
Side the head
From water-
Bed, from book of the dead
From gibbous to full
Moon, from cow jump over
The salty spoon.
From telephone call from
Paris, from Berlin, from Lynn,
from Duluth, from empty booth,
From forget me, from knot,
From 2 roads on the earth
Both taken from 2 tongues
Shaking from downside
Under, from bring home
The beacon, from Easter
From Ramadan, from Pesach from birth
From the air from what we share,
From our local quicksilver lair
From when you look at me
From when I look at you
From the door
From do you want more
From when we go home
We go home together

Two together
Gather roses / roses
Washed in the blood
Of the ordinary life

he called it
"a faraway country"

"When I go to the faraway country," Etheridge would often say, referring to his own death. We both knew what he was talking about. It made it easier for him to envision this journey he was preparing for, this journey that he didn't want to take. He said, when he heard he had terminal lung cancer, it felt like receiving a life sentence with no parole.

He preferred to cross borders. So, before he went to the faraway country, in the spring of 1990, we crossed over the northern border into Vancouver, Canada, and in the summer of 1990 we crossed the southern border from El Paso into Juarez, Mexico.

I remember Vancouver in April as being deep and green and lush. We stayed at the Sylvia Hotel near the bay on Stanley Park. We ate oysters and salmon and drank red wine from Washington vineyards and walked near the water and told the hard stories and asked the hard questions and laughed and cried a lot.

And talked more, and often said nothing at all. Etheridge kept smoking.

We went to the Anthropological Museum. We saw totems. We saw Creation Story carved out of wood. We saw raven and coyote and owl and fox. We saw a round opening where we could hear chanting, pulling us forward and through. Spirit life was opening to us. We felt it everywhere.

I was teaching poetry for Lesley College [now Lesley University], and Etheridge came with me to my Vancouver poetry class. There was a reading in town with, among others, Diane di Prima and Ted Joans. They asked Etheridge to join them. Eth was upset when they did not ask me to read. "Put Elizabeth up there. Her students come here tonight especially for her." He always advocated for me at times when he was the invited poet and I was not, just as he rejected what he called 'the New Yorker aesthetic' and the "artiste" persona. He quoted Carl Sandburg who said the word that should be eradicated from the language was "exclusivity." Eth said for him the word he wanted eradicated from the language was the word "hate." Poetry is all about freedom seeking," and that's all I have to say about that."

    Later on in August 1990 when I was teaching a poetry course for Lesley College in Las Cruces, we crossed the southern border into Mexico. Las Cruces New Mexico was hot and desert-dry with a flat cloudless sky. Things were moving inexorably toward what we could not see, but we knew would come. We drove by day through fields of onion and cotton. We whispered into sleepless nights. We went into Mexico for a day. Etheridge drank coronas and smoked, looked at the southwestern sky. Times were getting tougher, and the pain was getting sharper.

therapy

My friends
have a padded therapy room
in their basement
where they go
to be heard and healed
to shout
or blast the air
with their despair
And they do
And they get through (sometimes)
and the body sighs
and stops its lies
(for a while)
and smiles
and is released
at peace
(sometimes)

but you shake your head
and say:

I been in a padded room
It's called the Hole
No way of tellin'
The stink from the soul
No way of tellin'
The dark from the night
No way of tellin'
The demon from fright
No way of tellin'

The terror from tear

Thin | blanket | chill | stone
Slop | bucket | and
Me | all | alone
So that shout-healin' therapy
Don't work for me
'Cause the world
Is still out there
And we still ain't free

(and that's all I got to say about that)

the sack

From the sack
How much I wanted from you.
Important it was to me. How?
Understood. You knew how.
It again. Of course you.
I was called on to hear.
Died, I heard it! Then,
those in pain. Before,
I called out to all.
How much shone in there!
How much earned, how
much was sacrificed, how much
heard about,
which I had, often.
I loved the sack. How
near me, carrying
a large sack.

You were walking

a large sack.
near me, carrying.
How I loved the sack
which I had often
heard about,
how much was sacrificed,
how much was earned, how much
shone in there. I called out
to all in pain. Before I died
I heard it. Then I was called

*to hear it again. Of course
you understood. You knew
how important it was to me,
how much I wanted from you,
from the sack.*

Addiction Poem
Elizabeth Gordon McKim

[ketchup]

Ketchup

You took my car: the old chevy chevette we called TJ
Tough Joey into the hood to cop drugs
You called and told me you were on your way home
But the car was not. It had been stolen. You were crying.
You came back with a bouquet of daisies
And Deta Salomé was here and Sam Allen
You went into our bedroom and when I came in
You were praying... You were on your knees praying
You left for a poetry gig somewhere the next day.
Leaving me with no car
I called our friend Vance Gilbert
When the car was discovered by police
And had been removed to a tow place
In Roxbury. Vance came and helped me pick it up
I remember there was an attack dog.
A small wooden building.
When we got the car back it was
Slightly battered, and in the back seat
Was a black girdle and an empty
Box of French fries smeared with

Ketchup

Elizabeth Gordon McKim

from interview
"freedom and confinement"

(With Elizabeth Gordon McKim and Etheridge Knight)

Just being straight gave me a lot of emotional turmoil. I remember in the fifties, I'd say "I'm gonna give it up. Fuck this." Especially, if I'd just gotten busted. I'm gonna get me a job, and I'd spend the mornin' lookin' for a job. After two or three rejections, I'd go out and steal somethin' else. When I quit school, what I said to my old man, really to this day, ain't changed much. If you tell a little black boy: defer, work hard, follow all the rules, you can be president. You know it's a lie. Even today, I knew when I quit school my reasoning was, what the fuck good is this going to do me, and to tell the truth, I still believe that it's valid. Even now I don't believe the possibilities are great to develop into a citizen. No matter if you follow all the rules and work hard. I still don't believe a black man becomes a citizen, so what the fuck.

    I was already displaced. And I knew something was wrong without being able to verbalize it. I knew something was wrong. I knew that stealing and the way I was living was immoral. That's the way I felt. I understood all that. I'd learned that from my momma. Yet there was a drive, a pain. It's like having a toothache in your soul, in your psyche, and the drugs just deaden it. And after a while when you get hooked, it ain't the high that you're seekin', as much as the easin' of the pain. Just bein' fixed. They say 'getting' well.

betty blues

I say when my Betty left me
When she walked out the door
I say, she looked over her shoulder
Said, Man — I don't love you any more

And I cried, Lord Lord Lord
What's po' me gonna do —
I feel like water aint wet
I feel like the sky sho / aint blue

My baby shook one hip — And
Then she shook the / other
She said, I'm leaving lil boy
She said, I'm sending you back / to mother

And I cried, Lord, Lord, Lord
What's po' me gonna do
Cause I love that hip-shaking Betty
Like a clover bee loves the dew

       — *Etheridge Knight*

angel fish

And back to the angels
And back to the broken shards
And back to the opening door
And back to the invitation of the other
And back to the overwhelming odors
And back to the one who stands in the shadows
And says o door o door
And now under all this love and clutter
We find the possible poems
Hiding there
Waiting for you and me to claim them and ourselves
On and on into infinite surprises away from prying superiors
The raining up the falling away
The dark smudge of letters
The magic boy learning to read
Following the heroic adventures with his sweeping vision

And back to the call of the ravens
Their sleek backs on the tile grooves
And back to preoccupation in the nation
And back to the leaves of money waiting under the eves
So my advice to you
To whom I address these words
Is to continue
With the out / pouring
And just accept that you do not know
You do not know at all
What it means
And remember that
even when I am not here

And even when I die
You are my friend
And I will still be listening
listening
love
e/liz

forge

Deep inside
where you terrorized
our dwell
the one you shared
with drugs and deals and
dangers your old pals
in that place where you woke
unwell at night
to drive
into the soft shell
of my purse hoping to find some relief
to propel you far from grief
at the bank
light and weightless
did you feel the help-
less plight of my forged name
shot up high did you
feel it / gulp / in pain / cry / out / in fright /
i put in / you took out
2 poets on a spree / what response / ability /
do you take for me / for thee / for poetry
for men and women
you have loved / this wound / is real / it hurts /
it tears the web we live within / it knows
its way around our need
it stalks our neighborhood

Brookline, MA, 1988

hustler

Ruthless. Only out for himself when the drugs were talkin.'
    Didn't give a fuck who he hurt.
Whom. His mother. His sisters. His lovers. Closest friends.
    Nearest and dearest. People he lived with. *Kadoom.*

Worked the women. One against the other. So they'd fight.
    Turn on each other.
Black Woman. White Woman.
Pussy. Money. Work the women.
Learned it from the streets.
Works.

Robber. Thief. Pimp. Taker. Croaker. Toker. Maker.
Forger. User. Mean Misuser.
He knew it all. He knew what
he was capable of.
Buddies on the street knew too.

And lie? Swear on your mama's bible? "Anyone else want to
    cop out?"
He could make you lose your hold. "You don't have no money
    in your wallet.
You're mixed up. Con / fused.
Get it straight. No one stole your car.
There was no needle.
You're actin' crazy.
Crazy!"

You want danger? You want trouble?
You want damage to your life?
You got it.
Done.

                                            Brookline, MA, 1988

blues for the trouble maker

Who the hell / who the hell
do you think you are
This time you gone crazy
This time you gone too far

Everything calm and peaceful
Till you come along
Then you stir up my trouble
And all the rules are gone

Gone right out the window
Gone right into dark
Hear the babies cryin'
Hear the wild dogs bark

This is my boundary
And this is my frontier
Don't you dare cross over
And mess with my fury
and my fear

Gimme back my secrets
And gimme back my stuff
Haven't you had your fun with me
Haven't you had enough

Who the hell / who the hell
do you think you are
This time you gone crazy
This time you gone too far

notes for a play called the waitin' room

1. Prayer Circle
2. Dia carries knife behind his neck, between his shoulder blades in a scabbard. When he is very angry or tense, his right hand moves first to his chin, rubbing either it or stroking his mustache, then his hand moves to the back of his neck. When he begins to rub, massage the back of his neck, he is ready to strike. The gestures are recognized by only Charlene and Joyce, both of whom have seen him in action with the knife. He uses the knife three times in anteroom to vent anger and frustrations, 1. after argument with Dot, 2. after Laura's death near play's end, "He's either gonna kill Dot or start back shooting dope which is killing himself."

Three

and three
we don't know about
three we have lost
we can not figure out
we only know the knife is used again

could it be
when you Dia
lay dying and you found the knife in your half of the bed
and brandished it.

in my lover's house

I am never alone,
even when she's gone
she's near;
I carouse,
I dance among her things
Combs, shoes, rings
The waterbed we share
She sings in the air
Her presence's there
Her curtains are caresses
she sings in the air

Even the emptiness
of her purple blouse
lying wrinkled on the floor
I finger and feel her 'young girl's breast'

Her writing room, her center,
the creative chaos I dare not enter
without invitation to read a poem
or peruse a paper lest I somehow
rape her

In my Lover's House
I am never poor
In my Lover's House
I am never alone
Even when she's gone
She's here, humming in this air,
In my Lover's House
I am in her care

— *Etheridge Knight*

burial ground

1.

In sunlight
a safe spot

Put to rest in shade

and seeded
to be held

creatures
through all small

bends and arches

to be held
and seeded

put to rest in shade
a safe spot
in sunlight

2.

The cold stars
afterward
bloodroot
Falling through dogwood.

Our season. And the light

The long call —

Our season. And the light

Falling through dogwood.
bloodroot
afterward
the cold stars

3.

my body turns
in the clear focus of wind

I drink
of one mind with the body's heat
I touch into death
and the land's end

each turn of the wind
repeats

each turn of the wind

and the land's end
I touch into death
of one mind with the body's heat
I drink

in the clear focus of wind
my body turns

4.

Exploding

In the arms
asking
For nothing
Toward the river
Bending in animal silence
in silence
of animals
The sound. Over and over.
For nothing
asking

in the arms
asking
For nothing
of animals
The sound. Over and over.
of animals
in silence
Bending in animal silence
in silence
of animals
Toward the river

Exploding

waves

Written after Eth's death in March 1991.
Visiting my daughter in Puerto Rico. Staring at the ocean for hours.
Remembering the sounds as EK moved closer
to the faraway country.

that roiling sound

faraway faraway

where seas are made

can i comment on these furrows

These white foaming c's
rolling toward me as I sit
behind my tomorrows

these creatures of storm
foam / these moving battalions

relentless
in their motion

they do not pick up
on my sorrow

nothing like that

they keep to their own keening

a restless sobbing
in the winds

7

chapter

[out of the tunnel into the mississippi sun]

Out of the tunnel into the Mississippi sun
I have always been a lonely one
A lonely boy playing in the dust and shade,
A lonely brother, overpowered by two others,
encircled by four sisters, and a mother.

— *Etheridge Knight*

[this mountain is vast]

This mountain is vast
I search for the tiniest
    Pebble on the path

[when i slip to sleep]

When I slip to sleep
In spring, leaves will sing. Liz's
Fire'll seek another flame

        I think about my woman
        a lot now that I'm leaving for
        a faraway country

I hurt in certain
Places when the wind caves in
You die in my arms

        Black Bird I all ways
        Loved you. Wherever you chose
        To fly. Now call home.

— *Elizabetheridge*

CHAPTER 7
*Submerged and Found
The moon
A black face
In my mirror*

swallowing song

At first whole continents.
Archipelago. Savanna. Promontory. Great Plains. Delta.
Death valley. Northeast kingdom. Mississippi.
The great Missouri.
Juan de Fuca The Straits.
Swallow. Swallowing song
A way. Far off.
Bird early in the rising.
Owl. Raven. Cormorant.
The swallow.
sw sw
wallowing
tear crystal flake leaf speck dot
sw sw
winging
all
owing allowing
no thing st st
uck uck
only
this singular
song you are
singing

in the rising
muck

Creation: Vancouver Anthropological Museum

during the night

Awake three times.
Knock. Tremble. Entry.
What more could I want
Before dawn sweeps in
A diva in red
Bearing revelation
Like a ripe berry.

ride

those last days
you were all ways talking
about taking a ride
and mama and I joined you
in preparations
sooooo
miss belzora says
we gonna take a ride
down home
we gonna
take a ride
get us a big ol' caddy
an 'lizbeth
why she'll drive
and you and i
we'll sit in the backseat
and jes enjoy
the ride
oh yes
yes sirree
we will

for jenifer mckim

July 28, 1986

When I was twenty —
Like you;
I knew a plenty
That's true
And I too
Was full of breath

Now tho, I'm fifty-five,
Alive, and full of jive
And righteous rage
I yet bless the days.
I loathe death.

— *Etheridge Knight*

For Jennifer McKim:

When I was Twenty —
Like you;
I knew a plenty,
That's true.
And I too
Was full of breath.

Now tho, I'm fifty-five,
Alive, and full of jive
And righteous rage
I bless the days
I ~~find myself~~ feel alive.
I loathe death.

To Jennifer McKim
—Health/Love/Freedom,
—Etheridge

**POEMS
FROM
PRISON**

This is to let you know that as you wander /over Europe that you've got a Black Knight/Angel looking lovingly /over your shoulder.

o elizabeth

Woman of my wanderings —
Wife of my comings and goings —
Sister of my rap and rhyme,
I thank thee, goode Giver,
for the gift of Time and Tenderness,
You bless my 58th year, tho
I be / here / in this Domain
of Death and Excellent Pain
I languish. I suffer. I exalt —
Do you still love me? Is —
my smoke still in your
fire? How can you love me?
Me: liar cheater and dirty
mistreater / I love you
I, man of the high step
and the long-laugh.
Despite the rocks and
shoals and silver water
falls, our rivers flow
together. Who knows
what the weather / will
be tomorrow, We row
for sunshine, not storm,
We row for joy not sorrow

— *Etheridge Knight*

beyond words

There came the time
when you lost all language
tightly strung together
to be heard.
Encompassed.
Under / stood. The tops
left off the bottles.
Not purposefully.
Lapsed. Left un-
done in the awe / full light of a forgetful
sun weighting for some other earth
or ear / full. The sounds
moved rapidly toward soul / scat
somewhere close and faraway.
So it was justice and surprising
that the meanings and the words returned
like lovers after a fuss
unexpectedly and at important times
like when your sisters were in the room and you chanted
(out of the Oral Tradition) a poem of forgiveness
you repeated over and over
and the words came out as clear as knight
in a song you could have sung all day
as if suddenly
you remembered something painful
(like stealing the rent check
or searching the unattended purse)
and now you wanted, no needed, to clear
the tumbling tables.

I remember
I'm sorry
I remember
I'm sorry
I remember
I'm sorry

Or in the last minutes of the last morning
when you asked your Mama clear as any old day
you asked her to sing a hymn for you
and she sang *Jesus is on the Main Line*
and you asked her to pray for you
and she took your hand and prayed you down the ages
she prayed for Mama's manchild
body and the soul and then she left the room

and that is when you dropped like an egg on the horizon
into my arms and you started in to *Ride*

a few more minutes to live
and you knew what was after you
was no mean angel
you knew that *for real*
as your mama says
you knew that *truly*
as I say
and your eyes were so intent
fixed
and after all
you had already asked
your mama for a prayer
and she had sung
jesus is on the mainline

and your niece kasi had hung up a sign
WE LOVE YOU
so it was time to release
your convulsions
those all night agony sea-moans
that hurricane of sorrow
into morning conversions
and start
the RIDE
the lope across the bridge
the teeter on the ridge
the low / step the high / step
the RIDE
cross borders frontiers city limits
check point the corridor the take off
the departure
the whistle stop the siren
the ride

[taped to the wall of my cell]

Taped to the wall of my cell are 4 pictures.
The upper left is Elizabeth, the upper right
is my sister Clyneese, the lower left
is my mother and the lower right
is my father. My father is dead
but my mother is not, my sister lives
with my mother, and I live with Elizabeth
who is my lover.

Now I am alone.
I am a poet and a poem, a moaner
and a groaner, a weeper and a mid-
night creeper. I am a free man.
I'm my dead daddy and my living sons,
I'm a low / down lyin' / son-of-a-gun.
I'm a lover, I'm a hugger, I'm a
high stepping Free man, I'm a
worker, I'm a shirker, I'm a fucker, I'm a sucker,
I'm a crap-shooting lucker.

Each fall the voices of my ancestors
speak, and sing in the wind.
My dead brother and sister visited me.
She saved me from revolutionary retribution.
My brother was mute, powerless.
I am not he. I am She. She is
me. In my earlier life, I was betrayed
by my mother. She sent me away
and chose my brother.

— Etheridge Knight
MacDowell Colony

prison

No mobility: that's what he said:
the worst thing about prison
it takes away your mobility
when you are imprisoned
by the prison
system

so work the system / work / it
work it / any way you can

after a while he used it
like a college campus
he had a routine
he read at night with the light from the fish tank
he said that the little prison inside is connected to the
    big prison
outside... always the metaphors

when he was dying the cancer inside
was like the big cancer outside
Desert Storm
and after, Abu Ghraib
the photos the dogs the leashes the tortured
genitalia humiliation

What does it mean to be human
To be human to be human
Strung up prodded shamed
We send our human pearls to die in
Pools of degradation

habit

Food
Foo
she sez. Mik.
Mik. Mik. Mik. Mik.
Foo she sez
d she sez
Food. I'm fuckin'
you know stickin'
what / fed up.
Food
she sez.
Booze
she sez.
Brink she sez
Ink she sez. Home she sez
Polly wanna cracker
quaker / sucker / shaker / croaker / fucker

Suck / suck
Suck onna tittee of love
with your habit on

words of fire

sometimes
we need
a sword of fire
to say no
to say separate
to say cut
to say wait
to say hear
to say no more shit
to say this is it
to sting the air
to slice despair
to snap
to release
to sere
to say we
to say peace
words of fire
swords of fire
sometimes we need
a sword of fire
to say me / to
say thee
to say free to stay free

Guardian
Indianapolis, IN

Photo: Elizabeth Gordon McKim

chapter 8

Maybe I'll meet her in Denver
Maybe I'll meet her in the fall
Maybe I'll woo her and win her
Maybe I'll do nothing at all

— *Etheridge Knight*

angel

For Etheridge Knight

Well I really didn't want to approach this one
the huge one the high honcho
the big guy the cell boss of angels the one
I have been leaning / toward / leading / up to / the one
in the corner / the one who swoops / and flails / and flips
the one who veers / the one who means business
the workaholic one the one
who never goes to miami the one you knew was in the room
the one I knew was in the room the one who did not leave
the one you tried to smote the one i tried to smote
the one who finally wrapped wings around you
as you breathed your way into me convulsing
as you flew light and easy as you swarmed
out the window singing *ride ride*
no i am going to leave this
alone i am going
to stop here

singing

entries

Most of these journal entries were made in the hearted space between life and death: trying to give shape to the confusion going on around me and inside me during the last ten weeks of Etheridge's living and dying. I was not trying to make finished poems, nothing like that, but rather to name my experience simply and spontaneously, listening in on our lives. I usually wrote in the morning, and Etheridge liked to hear me working at my electric typewriter in the room next to the bedroom where he was drifting. It was important to him to know I was continuing to write. It was like his belief in the earth: everything spinning as usual and according to plan and prediction, change and continuance.

entry

Wanna know
what it's like
it's like getting a letter from a friend
you feel the person
through the words
that's what I want
simple
so we can all
understand
knowledge
the kind of knowledge
which is
always present
for us all

entry

Jan. 7, 1991

Yesterday we drove from Memphis
to Raimer Tennessee on the Mississippi / Tennesee / line
in a rented silver caddy
to pay respects to E.K.'s daddy

Etheridge Bushie Knight
1905-1950

We stop at the general store for directions
deer up to two hundred pounds weighed here
irs refunds paid here
chaw / tobacco / beef jerky
double / bubble / whisky

We find the cemetery
cross the tracks
past the creek
up the hill
to the part reserved
for colored
(white folks portion of the boneyard
distracted
and closer to the traffic)
This the quiet place
which looks out
on a pond in slumber

Cows graze here in summer

The stone is large and dignified

Etheridge Bushie Knight
1905-1950

Eth moves near
but not too near
bows his head / slant
feels what he comes to feel
does what he comes to do
then we get back
in the silver caddy
and drive back to Memphis
in the bitter rain
Eth now in deep
and unremitting pain
his hand on his burning liver
and his mind on his daddy

gotta watchout / gotta watchout
gotta watchout / for the ol' liver

we crawl into bed
at the Days Inn
hold tight and shiver
watch the senate hearings
on the gulf war
press on and on
we finally drop to sleep
close to Mississippi
in Memphis Tennessee
where the thin light screams
and dread is in the air we breathe

we breathe we breathe each other into dream

Bushie crossed the Tennessee / Mississippi line
he crossed it on a mule to court Belzora

Bake a lil' bread / tote a lil' water
Mama Mama can I marry your daughter

february 3, 1991

Waves uncurl
and curl
tides and winds
abide
ride the waves
till we can roll
no more
the moon costs nothing
and the sidewalk
50 cents
all that you have
I look for blossoms
coax our plants
the blooms hiding beneath
green leaves
peeking into
mottled light
pink and promising
crimson at the center
shaped like sails
winging it
lips / two lips
a flotilla of blossoms
we can only be grateful
filled full
pink promises on sturdy green
and deep down
brown

entry

Feb. 18, 1991

POETRY YOU SAY

1.

poetry
you say
a con-
coction of memory
imagination and ex-
perience
don't forget
magic
last night funky drum
came by with his wife
wanted some money
for the magic elixir
km
said he was now into multi-
level marketing
lots of changes
since you 2 partners
moved the hot air
conditioners
I told him you were sleeping
He said that's good —
That way you're on
Escape
Oh man

The trips we have taken
When I first met you
In Boston February 1981
In that old black fur like coat
You had almost died
In a fire
In Memphis
And the people
In the streets below
Shouting Poet Poet
and the landlady trying to wake you
and fanning the air
I could still smell
The smoke
Inside you
When we slid together
Into the crooked room
I knew I was crossing
A bridge
It called
like a siren
elizabetheridge
next morning
you said to me
lady I could ride the river
with you
all the way to the sea

listening in on eth

An Evocation: For Etheridge Knight

Woke up full of mississippi
the far cries, the farm, mama's animals
cows pigs chickens rabbits bitin' snakes intertwined
uncle cat eye hosie rosie aunt dink uncle pink
my cousins miss lilac lips
the old cars men always underneath 'em
shotgun house railroad flat rat titty chasin' big sis
clear through the rooms one after another and out
the far end. outdoor toilet.
doves. scratchgrass in the moonlight.
possum and coon. snakes in the red dust. you ain't better 'n
nobody else and nobody better 'n you.
Mama — teachin'. charles. floydell. me. clyneese. honey. dale. janice.
a stingin' in the blood as i walk along the road.
goin' home
with the song singin' in the blood.
mine flowin' out. stingin'
on the road between here and paducah and further.
always further
charles drove me to city limits dropped me off
do you really want to go junior he asks?
"take a train to chicago. kansas city too. see, see rider,
see what you done done"
red dust taste. it's the soup we sing on. neckbones and collard greens
ol' hound mouth. learned the songs from him
out on the streets in the parks
said them over and over / over / and over
never did subscribe to no rules. like be home by dark.

let the good times roll. down home. runnin' with the wild ones.
bleedin. hurtin' too. how should i have known.
the hole. the dry shave. the baseball bat.
head cracked open like a ripe melon.
no women to look to for comfort.
just the steel doors clangin' shut keys lockin' us in
maybe the guys from pendleton were right.
i am a low rider. c c rider. see what you done done
outside the nickel
in those last days. slidin' down the walls
on the hot nights when e was back in beantown
an ol' mr. k bottoming out
full of dark eyes and ol' man death close up on my neck hairs
my heart full desperation
fear of cessation and a lil' bit
of wonder. one two. buckle my sorry ass shoe
nobody's lookin' round now
'cept ol joe and fishface
down town and six feet under / you think it was a party
e when you first went to michigan city
asked about a prison wood shop like the one in thomaston maine
on the way to tenants harbor carved boats shiny polished boxes
rockin' chairs remember we are movin' closer
in up and around between beyond whichever way we turn
you'll find me dawgin' you... i told you so

entry

The days roll in and out in waves
Eth sleeps and eats and wakes and sleeps again
It is quiet in the apartment
Tandi came by this afternoon for a visit
The sun had been out all day
light pouring in the window
snow / slush outside
Phone keeps ringing then we take it off the hook
Minimal activity seems right for the hibernation time
I have decided to postpone my trip
to visit my Jenny girl even though I miss her so
This seems to be the only place to be
I told Miss Belzora
She asked me
If I wanted to go home and rest up
I said no this is where I want to be
She understood she got it
Days later she came to live with us
Her grandson Winky brought her clothes
In a shopping cart with food
The war rages on
I wonder if it will ever be over
Now that it has been fifteen days
I can not remember any time we did not have a war
It seeps into everything we do

into the food we eat
the water too
images that lie in our dreams
meaning fear meaning war

so many losses seeping in
the sad time
the closet the closing
faces cracked and howling
we lay in wait for some relief
Deta Salomé sings sireens in the night
Roberta Flack sings the first time ever i saw your face
and we feel full with feeling
we hold each other and cry
sorties and scuds / sorties and scuds
what do we know we did not know before
they drop the bombs with laser beam accuracy
new born babies howl
angel wings flap like laundry on the line
stay at home with my love is all I want to do
and keep my body open and healthy

so why am I smoking?

last stand

Feb. 5, 1991

foggy day
in ol' indy town
a sad sheet of sadness
washed away and washed over
the war rages on and on
bombs found attached to tanks of dangerous materials
in norfolk virginia
breathe breathe *remember the member*
so often I soften
and we move through and on
this fog / this fog
don't know why I feel so shaky today
is it because eth is in such pain / such pain
raw / war / raw / war
last night we watched custers last stand on tv
the falling away
the battle
please mr custer i don't wanna go
pray pray
for the days to come
o lord give me strength
eth woke up this morning in great pain
in great pain / his liver burning up
unanswered whirling questions
why did the house burn
why does the daughter cry
as the world rages
what a world we live in now

precarious my best belief
take it in
close it up
wrap it up
sign off
good by
so long sayonara
adios see ya
adieu
put the top back on the bottle
close the closet door
put the cap back on the toothpaste
shut the bureau drawer.
forever and ever
amen
Ready for war. Or more.

sunday morning

1.

king hussein of jordan
says his country will not be bought
with american money
'we are not that cheap' he says
a man with integrity
wholeness
a precious quality

i don't want to fast
but i keep finding
myself / fasting
fast
hold fast

**as missiles streak
circles / appear
and disappear
reappearing**

I bought a gardenia plant

It has at least five
furled blossoms
I want to bloom
petals hot and moist

I remember my daughter
In mexico

in oaxaca plaza
and each night
we bought corsages
of the tropical
gardenia

*what do we know
we did not know before*

ride the river

Feb. 20, 1991 entry

Lies and mis / demeanors
violations and manipulations
minor and major thefts
curl and uncurl
in the tides
and the winds pick them up
and blow them out to sea

a long time ago
after the first time we made love
you said to me
i could ride the river with you lady
all the way to the sea
and you are a man who knows the river
and I am a woman who knows the sea
I grew with it
it taught me when i was a little girl
it rose and fell with me
i knew its storms and calm
its grey days
its bright mornings
when sunpennies dance on the waves
i know ancient tide / pools
little wonder / worlds
when chinamen caps barnacles periwinkles
sleep in a kelp kingdom
i studied the granite rocks
their steadfast postures

    their scars and creasings
        their warnings
    their strange earth-alphabet

last free peoples

steve stoller speaks
of free peoples poetry
getting the word out
a commitment
to peaceful engagement with others
dismantle the military complex
share resources
for food and shelter the rearing
of children taking care
of elderly
and peaceful pursuits
of life and art
protect the space
in the spirit of the free peoples poetry
eth listens quietly
and returns to bed
we talk of practical matters
a space and place for free peoples
to be / and breathe
and share the circling
revolution
the evolution
of an idea
from one leaf to another
from one leaf
to its brother
then we read some poems
and a long beautiful story
by Herman
about an old farmer

facing a grave illness
and the possibility of losing his farm
Francie reads her poem
about the bridge
of oil and water
and the pulling together of wood
and Sonny is hurting badly
from a tooth
just extracted
the pain of what has been taken
out / and the first day
without the old job
time to concentrate on new
work. Then JT arrived
read his strong haiku
about the war situation
and i read yesterday's entry
from my journal
pages and pages
of what is pouring
out of me
outpouring

haiku

Clouds and Mountains merge
Above the Bay in North Vancouver
We rue the Rain

O Haida totems!
Tall totems-totems small-O!
All / we / be totems!

                 — *Etheridge Knight*

Drawing and haiku by Etheridge Knight

9
chapter

entry

Jan. 28, 1991

A ma / zing morning spreads
out over
indy town
a wide sweep of blue
pushing through

francie steve and bam here
circling round and round
tellin' tales
francie tells us liver remedies
she has studied all night
and her knowledge pours out
like a wise old biblical woman
shawl'd babuska'd
she knows wise teachings
rumbled and roiled
in the body's soul and soil
steve sits quietly
listening talking softly to bambata
letting the talk roll gently
up down and all around
etheridge / as he sleeps
and sculpts the air
with his hands
and the deep cadence
of his voice groaning
out and out and in again
moving over the swells

the heave and the rise
the pulling back
the pushing
forward
what do we know
we did not know before

i know before you tell me
a death is like a birth
out and out
don't look back
to what we come home to:
the light and dark simplicities
the deep
listening
lightening
the spaces

death / breath

Is this about the in / take
or the ex / hale?
Is this about the going out
Or the coming in
Is this about the moment
between
the flutter / ring
the pulse / sing
or the convulse / sing?
Is this about the singing
or the stinging

Is this about the wrong / doing
or the well / being
is this about vision
or re / vision

version or con / version
Is this about for / giving?

we / be / runners –
we / free / runners

HE:

I dream of running
And flying.

I could be fairy
Or a flag
Dia Ajanaku on the warpath

I run, I run, I run
With a white / girl, who
Does not have a curl
In the middle of her forest.
She has a cabin,
Where there is warmth
And light, and wisdom.
I am brave.
I visit her cave,

In the night,
Or in the day,
And we play parents.
WE fly far
WE flee fast
WE dream dreams that last

SHE:

My father is a fellow

Who does not falter
He cuts brush
In the Fall
And
Fends
For us ALL.
Then,
There came this man,
Shiny and as black
As a can of oil.
He made my blood bubble and boil
And blushed my cheeks with heat.
He was neat,
A veritable "Peter Wheatstraw"
The Devil's Son in Law,
But I luuuuuuuuve him.
We fly, even when he's falling.

— *Etheridge Knight*

Found in a tablet of construction paper, Jan. 1991.

sampson snake root

Feb. 5, 1991

"I'm gonna take you out to lunch
where you ain't never been before — " you said
"And make it good — " I said
You took me down beside the Frosty Tap
where weary men and women wait
for Meals on Wheels and a prayer
for precious lord and we got lunch

*and now you're on the way
to some place far away
so when you get there
find a place for me
and make it good.*

Today is Monday
the day I was supposed to go
to Puerto Rico
to visit my Jenny girl
and here i am
in Indy town
the war still
raging.

Yesterday we went to Miss Belzora's for lunch
I took a long walk down North Dexter and Harding and beyond
in the surprising February thaw.
People out washing cars. Kids on bikes.
Guys calling out from street corners.

People sitting on wide front Indiana porches.
Etheridge is sleeping almost full time now
except for meals.
I talk a long time to his mama.
She tells me of auntie and her medicines

tansey root / peach leaves
cherry bark / palm lilies
sampson snake root
from the tree's north side
and the special dark mixture
for the bad disease
a man gets from a woman
or a woman from a man

We come home to the nickel
watch custer's
last stand on tv
fall asleep early
while the war still rages

Sampson snake root
Sampson snake root

february, 1991

for EK

In our room I hold
you in the light left to us
you fall across me

When the world enters
us both we let go hold on
two small animals

Our bodies cry out
through the long night and out in-
to the next thresh hold

february 7, 1991

woke early.
couldn't sleep
we had a quiet 'family' free people's poetry workshop last night
herman and francy and steve and jean
and susan neville who is writing
an article for arts indiana
and eth
so sick and tired tonight
he stayed in bed.
I bought a cyclamen today
bright pink blossoms like crimson sails
boats of the dream
growing things
I need growing things
I am tired
as if this is
"the dead of winter"
so many parts of our routine
falling, falling away
jazz / trips to the chatterbox / the walker casino
sunset lounge / daily trips to the stoller gallery / sundays
    at mama's
frosty tap / jwhit's for groceries

All falls away
In the sieve of wind

We cleave to each other
And let go

All falls away
But love

Our skin
Like parchment promises

fog clarity

Feb. 9, 1991

It's clear
even in the fog
this is no damn time
to be blue'
'cause we be pushing through
at dawn we wake and talk
of noise and sound and space and beat
the world of heated differences between
a and the
as in a love of my life or the love of my life
and listening to the inner voice
and circulatin' haints
and the heat of eth's ol' liver
eth says he ain't got no more time
he moves instead through sireens in the night
with Chance
with a big C
same like cancer
but way different
whereas me
I live among the churn and weave
of cloud and wave
under a bucket of blue
what to do
what to do
burnin'
burning through

sirens in the night

Feb. 10, 1991

everything affects us
air raids sirens in the night
scud attacks and anti missile
missiles pows oil spills landings
counter landings sightings
eth so tired now
heavy with fatigue
tired of the relentless pain
he can not muster
enthusiasm for the journey ahead
postures and pictures
near misses
twists of fate
never too late
letting us down
putting up
with or without
stop the war
raw
wear it down
go to bed
not on your head
fall out of bed
call the doc
bury the rock
give it up
fuss the brother
call up the mother

call down the father
consult with jah
bring in ra

my ma who is eighty four
and has lived through five wars
says take the toys
away from the boys
let the women decide
if we should start a war
or not
tangle with history
wrangle with destiny
let it go
the snow is melting
it is time to sleep

can we muster enough energy
to take the ride
or let it be
the sea invents
the tides
we slide and grope
more rope more
rope a picture of despair
no no let it go

let the rain decide
where
we glide
another time
another time

february 11, 1991

chants on the tape
over and over
the sweet repetitions
so simple
creation stories spinning
around me
the light falls on the gardenia plant
relevant
circumvent
hyper / ventilate
egregiously
deep / into the river
repetitions
so many we have seen
mississippi charles farmington
ganges rio grande
the migrant workers from juarez
wading across
the rio grande
to el paso
wading across
the mississippi wide
bloated with old
stories
flooding its banks

river / maid seine of the old town
ganges filled with bodies
holy cows and small pox victims

we sit in the place of the sacred burial ground
the sweetness of life overwhelms

february 14, 1991
valentine's day,
indianapolis

I am very tired
my body putting forth its complaints
at night I lie
beached and dry
next to eth
i put my hand on his chest
and feel *the in and out*
in / in and out
that's the way the poem begins
and then i put my hand on his liver
it feels hard and large and hot
i stroke his forearm
he moans in his sleep / wakes / wants water
falls back to sleep
we are both tired
Francy continues to research cancer remedies
she was on the phone for four hours yesterday
Sonny Bates came by in the afternoon
we talk in the living room about his future
jobless for a while and wanting to poet
we talk of love and sex and marriage and children
and what it means to be a twenty seven year old blk male
poet in america he brought us one yellow rose
I put it on the new bedside table
that Miss Belzora brought over yesterday
Bam came over later
we talk
the most amazing thing is that

he calls Mary McAnally Eth's second wife she asks to speak to me
I talk to Mary McAnally
for the first time in almost ten years
I woke early this morning
Tomorrow I fly to Reno to teach

new hampshire

Entry, Feb. 22, 1991

gathering and sifting
gathering and sifting
that's what I do
that's what I do today
that's what I do

Outside the gulf war still rages
saddam and george
going at it
on the ground soldiers wait
hunkered down bunkered down
scud attacks on saudi arabia and israel
we get so little truth
outside this window
the american flag flaps
in the distance
in the foreground
the star and crescent
the sword
from the murat temple
prayers and chants
jokes and curses
smallsongs
re / member o re / member
my dreams were of dancing
when i was ten
my smoke is in your fire
Dennis here in the nickel comes by

in his wheelchair
'I don't want to be any-
where you ain't
and that's the truth,' he says to Eth
'Get me a cup' he says
I pick the beautiful
ceramic brown cup
the one we bought
from the woman on the third floor
he drops his cigarette in it
the smoke circles out
'See this cup?' Dennis says
Eth cocks an eye
'See that smoke?' he says
'That's your spirit,' he says
'and the cup is your body.
The smoke will be here
long after your body is gone.
You open the door and
you pass through'
Yesterday
Tim stopped by
in his wheelchair
'Don't get up
to the eighteenth floor much
Don't like heights' he said
'but I wanted to holler atcha, man
see how you was doin'
I've cleaned up my act
no booze no dope no sugar
got high blood pressure
sugar diabetes you know
got to watch it now.'

Sky is wide and clear today
no clouds
just a wide sweep
Remember o remember
the stand of birches in dublin new hampshire
we called those trees 'the ladies'
told stories about 'em
Imagined they told stories about us
'the thang' and his woman
we had found an unidentified
black object on a country road
in new hampshire
and we started telling these tales about
'her and the thang'
and how the ladies gossiped up there on the hill
even when the new hampshire pines shushed them
still those birches babbled on
spreading their malicious foolishness
over the cold sharp hills
and all the world surrounding
rounding the bend
and it is true
that down in the village
cars would screech
and people would gawk sometimes
as we walked by and one time
Eth and I went into the post office
to mail a poetry manuscript of mine
to a literary competition
it was a thick-walled package
Secure as a uterus
carefully addressed
and when I got back to boston

the outside bag had been cut open
another book slipped in
a book by norman vincent peale
it looked like the bag had been stepped on
muddied with a boot
and returned to boston
the outside bag gone
the inside one
slashed with a sharp object
ah new hampshire
live free or die

when i hold you dying

*I learn
that breathing in
is a kind of birth into
the body
and breathing out
is a birth
into the uni / verse
the one verse
a continuous rhythm
in and out
in / in and out
I hold you from behind
With my arms around you
My hands on your heart
You birth into me
As you die
And
I live into you
as you birth into death
your weight finally flopping like a fish into my arms your breathing
light and lighter still
we are in the shallows now
as you leave the water
and make your way to the faraway country
your gasps and convulsions
moving into me
rhythmically
as I breathe into you
and you breathe out
into the big sea of silence
where I cannot follow*

having come this far away

I watch the knight skies
For signs
Steve says
You have become
A star

Waves appear
Relentless c's of rest
And restless
Distress

Thank you
For everything
Blazing

I pull toward earth
Splitting atoms
Tomtoms / tomes / stars
Rats / rattles
Re / membering you
Bit / by / little bit

seeing my dead lover in a dream

He was un / dressing
In the house of many rooms —
I saw right through him

chapter 10

a lil' hope is all we need

little hope
return and turn
surround us
with thy sweet blessings
little hope
sweet hope
your simple feet
on the good ground
we need thee
in our home
we love thee
and beseech thy grace
for us
your humble servants
we need thee
in our home
we love thee
on this earth
dance for us
slow and easy
slow and easy
little hope
come on with it
give it up give it out
for a long time
for a good long time
in our home
and the city which surrounds us
give us thy cornucopia
of harvest blessings

little hope
sweet home
grand and magnificent
small and unseen
we feel your heat and light
through the daze and knight
we love thee
all / ways — all / days
all / ways — all / days

— *Elizabetheridge*

Eth and I made this poem as a prayer for our home 555 Massachusetts Avenue Indianapolis, Indiana "Triple Nickel." We posted it by the doorway. We both contributed to it. I started it. He changed it. So it was Our Prayer.

entry

and the magnitude
of our life
and death
oh man
now we in the long run
haulin' up the mornin'
so many things to remember
to keep track
trackings
i'm dawgin' ya man
as you dawgin' me

haulin' up the mornin'
haulin' down the night

feb 18th home from reno
pick eth up at belzora's
eth says he wants to die in 555
miss belzora moves in
25 feb sonia's visit
deta arrives march 1
pills stolen march 3

friday 22/23 tandi's birthday

sunday dale's play
thursday march 7, first convulsion
dr sylvia dennison comes
judy van hoy
friday 8th all the ministers

march 10th
the day you caught the freight
byeeeeeeee
eeee
i'm outta here

[lean close to earth]

Lean close to earth. Feel
lost leaf tremble in a sling
of last summer's grass

pass / over

For Etheridge Knight
1931 – 1991

I asked you to come to me
and you arrived
I asked you to remember
My mother and you remembered
my mother
What more can come to me
from across the border
Thank you for
Every thing blazing
All day you have called to me
and all day I have answered

Photo: *Elizabeth Gordon McKim*

Photo: Etheridge Knight

song snippets

hush now
doncha cry
your mama loves you
by and by

simple man
and simple woman
sittin' in the simple sun
waitin' for the simple night
when they can have
that simple fun
Oh my lover
let me linger
in the
lap of love
ooowheeee
baby

one step
give us power
toward the light
and toward
the dark
one step
to give us power
toward the light
and toward
the dark
one step
one step

Even separation
Is a port of love
Oowhee baby

Photo: Etheridge Knight

        And continue on and on
        To the end of time
        Oh yeah

[the way he peers in]

The way he peers in —
to the open cups of light
The tulip lover!

song

the root is part of the flower
the flower is part of the root

the moon belongs to the water
the water belongs to the moon

the dark earth belongs to the sunlight
the sunlight belongs to the ground

the sound belongs to the silence
the silence belongs to the sound

faraway

In our dreams
   we see ourselves
      as sky-blue
  winged creatures

we dance face to face
       repeatedly
   touching
    each other
    with our mouths
  when it is time
   we begin our journey
  toward the sun
   sailing in the sky
      above
  the waves
by day and night
     effortlessly
  and almost
  without moving
    we come
   to rest
    only at
  nesting time.

having come this far
passing on

Has to go further further than even she remembered
   or dreamt in the dreamtime
      passed sage passed pignon past the widest
         sky her compañero de la vida calls the bucket of blue
            past adobe past mister past noon past arroyo past
               sorrow passed
                  sister passed streets passed coyote grinning ear to
                     trickster ear
passed four directions passed nighttime passed bear passed eagle
   passed death and its driving passed danger and weathers
      passed fur and wild feathers past fetish
         passed dancing past dread its arriving
            past tears past breath and its bearing past
eth past edge past ether past ridge past either
   passed ore past bridge

      now / ow / oh / no / one / won

past breath / past bet / past beth / past ee
   past liza / past knight / past love
      past lore / past now / past elizabetheridge
   past howling and crying / past sighing
      and stealing / past mister / past mercy / past reeling
   past k / past song and its stinging
      past reeling / past midnight and keening
past light / and its passing / past knight
   and his riding toward freedom
      his striding toward stretching our reaching with feeling
         our seeking toward freedom / toward freedom

deathrow

*"Well, they burned tough Tony last night
The man who didn't know the meaning of fright"*

Today's June first, today I go —
Today's my turn / to be / the star of the show
First comes Jojo, then Big Red —
But the main event's over, after I'm dead.
There'll / be / lights, and cameras, — and plenty action —
And ol' Mr. K. the main attraction.
There won't / be / no crying or copping no pleas,
Hanging on the bars or begging on my knees.
When it comes to / me / to walk the last mile —
I'll hold my head high — even wear a smile.

— Traditional (version, EK) June 1, 1983

That's all, folks!

song

Where / is / the brother
Of breathing / I wonder
And where / is / the sister
    — Of starlight

Why is / the darkness
Approaching the meadow
And where / is / the moon
    In the sunlight?

infant

A long journey.
Home or elsewhere. Pre-verbal
Mutterings. Languor.
I climb to where you are.
Clouds empty.
With a whole life ahead.

you looked at me and spoke so clearly k

Compañero de la vida says to me sweetheart
there is no end and no beginning to this busyness
motion / commotion / lifing / poeting / there is no end
it just keeps on going / on and on / forever and ever
ah men and women / why / every little thing including me
just keeps on keepin' on / forever and ever / i am still
traveling out into the cosmos / believe it / into
particles of space and light / into the night / into
the daze / ahmen and women / into the cornfields into
radical bodegas / into the flatiron / pawnshops into
the memphis poolrooms / into my heart / lapping your
shores / leaping / into the worn air hovering above the earth
tired and panting / still breathing / into damp babies
newly arrived / into the tired feet of workers / into
the kernel bursting the orange / into blossom / into bet
into sun / into blue screen / strange scream of life keeps on keepin' on

february, 1989

*Leaving AWP conference
and visiting EK
somewhere nearby*

I walked into
the room of bandages
there was a pale light
intruding
you lay on the bed
swaddled
your fingernails had grown long
your wounded hands
were like paws now
and the patch of skin removed
on your thigh was red and sore
what could I say
what could I do
but take off my shoes
and lie beside you on the bed
and sigh
Life is so short
I saw my daddy die
I was there when he moved into
An other province
we did not talk about the robbery
about the anger and the pain
we breathed together
in the February room
I remembered and recovered
the taste and touch and smell
of your body

lying close to you
one animal close to another

We are
2 small animals
moving
in this life
the only life
we know

this is an event of hearts

Where brothers and sisters insist their way
Down the avenues of love
Their mouths overwhelmed with song:
Freedom / freedom and fame
Freedom and pain
This is rain
And a river of people move all the way to the sea
Where streets / intersect / inner music connects /
With outer commotion / motion / sweet lullabies
Toasts / tremblings / deep body sighs / longings
Colors: gold white brown red black
A call / a gesture / a greeting
Shouts / sirens / laughter
A meeting / a community surrounding
Rounding the bend / mend / an end / and
A beginning / wishing / accomplishing
A grin and a grace of whirling
A bridge we have to cross over
Calling blackness back from disbelievers
The messages come / sparks deliver /
Words and pictures we need
Our bodies unfurl / we boogie down
The endless avenues of love
We are scared and scared
We are scarred and scared
We are scared and sacred
In the hoop of the world
And the green goes over and over

acknowledgments

elizab ETH eridge

When I arrived here
I saw you on the first landing
Grinning into the after-life
You are a hard act
To swallow or
Follow

Your belief. Your rhythm. Your pulse. Your panic. Your hearted
Belly laughter. Your stay at home pleasure / pain. Your know-
How / Your little / place / big / place / your prison /
Your solitary / your cranium / your voice / your bridge
We are standing under all the way to
Glitten. Your southern song
Your devious trickster ways
Your profound intelligences
Your agility your inclusion your
Teaching your hard
Rock your Mississippi
Blues your Tennessee
Waltz. Your
True

We Free Peoples Be Baby
We free peoples be...

Big thanks to poet Norman Minnick
my gifted Editor true blue at KC Press
and poet publisher Chris Jansen who first saw this manuscript at

the Great Mother Conference in Maine with Robert Bly and now... here comes... ETH...

I'm grateful to Kinchafoonee Creek Press, Athens Georgia

Thanks to my communities of family friends students compañeras compañeros teachers children writers artists renegades and wranglers... Thanks to rock poet Dr. Bob Bradley beyond oratorio / loving praises Danielle LeGros Georges / poetry angel / to Judith Steinbergh dearest friend and poet-teacher / all ways thank Steve Levine who sings on and on and to Elle Levine visionary painter, and Judith Greer Essex, San Diego my womantoree and her journal *Illuminations* and Wes Chester eco-poet singer song writer...

And to Margo Fuchs Knill poet of resilience and Paolo J Knill my performing partner who never forsakes and laughs at my jokes, and Poet-Teacher MP Carver my incomparable editor of *Lovers in the Free Fall* / to Poet Marge Piercy and David Ira Wood / and Lisa Graziano and Tobias Steed, Publishers and Editors at Leapfrog Press. And hearted thanks all ways to European Graduate School in Saas-Fee Switzerland and the Zurbriggen Family for so many years of hospitality and grateful always for almost fifty years at Lesley University in Expressive Arts and Creative Arts in Learning / and thanks to Lynn, Massachusetts, USA: City of poets writers and musicians and the Walnut Street Café in Lynn: Jim Chalmers proprietor and Tony Toledo, Don White, Theresa E McDermott White, Kato Walsh, Lisa Haley, Patty Punch, Alicia Churchill and many others, thanks to trance dancer Paul Senn and artist Tatiana Sloutsky and poet host Dave Somerset and music man T Max / and to the New England Poetry Club: thanks for awarding me inaugural Sam Cornish Award 2022 alongside Askia Touré / and thanks MCC for Cultural Sector

Recovery for Individuals Grant 2022 and thanks to my first family / daughter Jenifer McKim journalist extra / ordinary always providing mortar that keeps things together and gets things done, Jim Jepsen her literary husband who cooks with magic and reads *Ulysses* with his son Max, and for Chloe Elizabeth Jepsen at College de Science Politique de Paris who studies to make this shell-shocked world a safer place and Max my grandson at Harvard leaning into world literature and jazz hip hop and beyond... and for my sister painter Mimo Gordon Riley and David Riley who add flavor to creativity soup and all praises be: Free Peoples diaspora once upon a time and onward no telling where...

To the Great Mother community...

And all ways grateful to the Knight family Hanako Gavia, Floyd Knight Jr, Floyd Knight III, Clyneese Bennett, Janice Knight Mooney, Eunice "Dale" Bowens, in memoriam, and to Mary Tandiwe McAnally, daughter of my heart and the memory of her brother Etheridge Bambata McAnally, and enduring love to Miss Belzora Cozart Knight Taylor, EK's mother, and his father Etheridge "BuShie" Knight... with respect, love / and freedom seeking

To poets: Sterling Plumpp, Eugene Redmond, Yusef Komunyakaa, Robert Bly, Donald Hall, Galway Kinnell, Reginald Dwayne Betts, Terrance Hayes, John Murillo, Sonny Bates, Michael L.L. Collins, Robert Carr, Fran Quinn, Kenny Washington, Michael S. Collins, Charles Coe, Lamont Steptoe, Dennis Brutus, Ifyeani Menkiti, Thomas Sayers Ellis, Ethelbert Miller, Afaa Michael Weaver, Dan Carpenter, James Taylor, Tomas O'Leary, Jim Watt, Robert Smyth, Ron Price, Coleman Barks, Joel Lipman, Nick Muksa, Kenneth May, Michael Siegell, Steve Levine, Kevin Gallagher: all guardians at the gate.

And to the women with thanks: Sonia Sanchez, Charleen Blackburn, Carol Ann Robertson, Marge Piercy, Toi Dericotte, Carolyn Forché, Naomi Shihab Nye, Madeline Tiger Bass, Maxine Yalovitz-Blankenship, Judith Minty, Francy Stoller, Lynne Red Walker, Marilou Awiakta, Nikki Giovanni, Sharan Strange, Eleanor Wilner, Judith Steinbergh, Akiba Shabazz, Susan Neville, Deta Salomé Galloway, Gwendolyn Brooks, Karen Moss, Lakshmi Mudunurri, Priscilla Sanville, Georgia Popoff, Ellie Slade, Priscilla Sanville, Mary Buchinger Bodwell, Evelyn Kellum, Ruth Lefkowitz, and Norma Canner my womantor...

And for the little old lady in sneakers who stood up at my reading and actually applauded.

For the ones not named: Especially for you.

If you think
This love poem is for you
You are wrong
If you think
This love poems is for you
You are right
It is for all of us
Who breathe into each other's life
And stand alone.
See us we are the ones in the corner
We are the ones in the center
Here: someone is laughing
There: someone is crying
What difference does it make
It is for me it is for you
If you think this love poem is for you

— e/liz   3/18/23

The text is Freight,
designed by Joshua Darden
and published through
GarageFonts in 2005.
It was inspired
by the "Dutch taste"
school of typeface design.
Darden is the first known
African American
typeface designer.

¶

The titles are set
in Walkway,
an elegant sans serif
typeface designed by
Graham Meade.

¶

This book was designed
by Norman Minnick.

www.ingramcontent.com/pod-product-compliance
Lightning Source LLC
Chambersburg PA
CBHW071235070526
44583CB00017B/2186